A HOP THROUGH
AUSTRALIA'S HISTORY

Hop through two hundred years of epic effort and heroic deeds in less than a hundred minutes.

Funny, factual and fast.

Journey through Australia's unique history with Robert Treborlang's delightful rhymer-primer of easy-to-read, easy-to-remember facts.

From Captain Phillip's bid to start a new world to Paul Keating's bid for a republic, the book covers some of the more fascinating episodes of our past.

Terrifying tortures, assassination attempts, military campaigns, bankruptcies, the fight for women's vote, tragic explorers, aboriginal rebels, foreign spies, desperate bushrangers, all make an appearance in witty, concise and easy-to-remember rhymes.

Spontaneous and provocative, often dazzlingly simple, Mark Knight's illustrations open up a whole new way of looking at Australian history.

(This is a scary insight into the Australian sense of humour.)

Also by Robert Treborlang:

Books:
How to Survive Australia
How to be Normal in Australia
How to Make it Big in Australia
Staying Sane in Australia
Sydney, Discover the City
She Vomits Like A Lady
Men, Women And Other Necessities
How to Mate in Australia

Plays:
The Moon at Midday
The Messiah in London
Mr. Mendelssohn Presents His Oratorio `Elijah'
Fool's Gold (*with Ian Stocks*)
Obsessive Behaviour in Small Spaces (*with Ian Stocks*)
The Daisy Chain Gang

A HOP THROUGH AUSTRALIA'S HISTORY

Robert Treborlang

Illustrations by Mark Knight

MAJOR MITCHELL PRESS

Moi Moi made me do it.

First published November, 1993

Major Mitchell Press Pty Limited
P.O. Box 997, Potts Point
2011, Australia

Copyright (c) Robert Treborlang
Edited by Derek Hornsey
Cover and illustrations by Mark Knight
Printed by the McPherson's Printing Group

National Library of Australia
Cataloguing-in-Publication Data:
Treborlang, Robert
A Hop Through Australia's History
ISBN 1-875614 05 2
1. Australia - History - Poetry.
2. Australia - History - Humour.
I. Knight, Mark. II. Title.
994.00207

All rights reserved. No part of this book may be reproduced, stored in a retrieval system, or transmitted in any form, or by any means, electronic, mechanical, photocopying, recording or otherwise without the prior written permission of the Publisher.

CONTENTS

Fast Foreword	9
Our Good Old Discoverers	10
The Incredible Hulks	11
All Aboard	13
The First Fleet Statistics	15
Australia Day	17
Australia Night	19
The Year of Hunger	23
Aboriginal Rebels	26
The Castle Hill Uprising	27
The "Rum" Rebellion	28
Billy Bligh	31
Home on the Sheep's Back	32
The Bigge Report	34
Terror Australis	35
She'll be Apples	38
John Batman	40
Myall Creek	42
Billy Charles Wentworth	45
Caroline Chisholm	47
Ludwig Leichhardt	49
Ten Little Governors	50

Victorian Gold	51
The Eureka Stockade	54
Burke & Wills & Wright & Brahe	56
The Royal Visit	58
The Man in the Iron Cask	60
War in the Sudan	63
The Great Maritime Strike	65
The Crash of the 1890's	66
Lawrence Hargrave	68
Women Fight for the Vote	71
We're off to kill the Boers	73
Dr Quick	75
Mabel Was I Ere I Saw Melba	78
Gallipoli	80
So told me Mrs Dunn	83
Poor Henry	85
Charles Kingsford Smith	89
The Sydney Harbour Bridge	90
Jack and the Lions	91
Phar Lap: The Phacts	92
Donald Bradman	97
Pig Iron Bob	99
The Bombing of the North	100
Ming	103
Thomas Austin, Jean McNamara & The Hundred Year War	104
When the Face on the Money was Here	109
The Petrov Affair	110

Contents

The Strange History of the Liberal Party	113
Albert Namatjira	115
Jorg Utzon and the Opera House	116
Our Dawn	118
The Snowy Man	119
The Vietnam War	121
The Whitlam Sacking	123
End of the White Australia Policy	125
The Dingo's Christmas	128
That Year	130
Liberal Leaders	132
Keating's Lament	133
The Twelve Sons of Mother Labor	134
Dancing the Mabo	136
Aussie Keating goes A-cleaning	137
The Pest Poem	139
Republic Bid 2000	141
Anthem	143

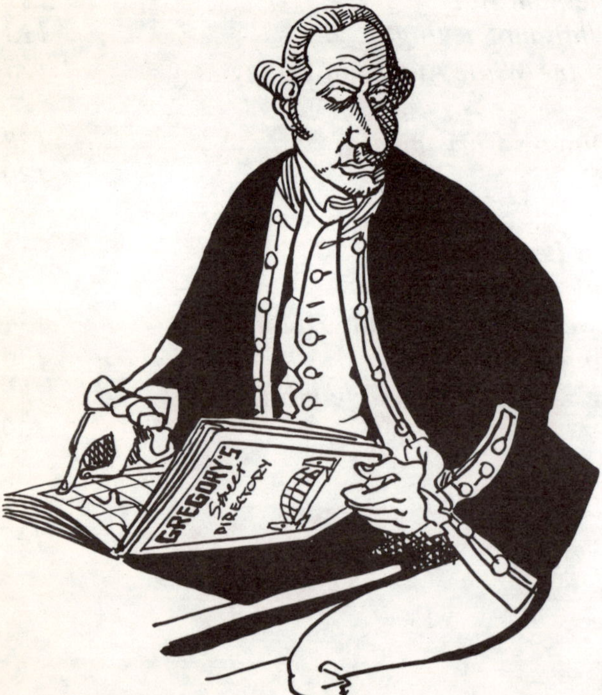
GREGORY'S
Street
DIRECTORY

FAST FOREWORD

The English count their days from Caesar,
Americans from their Mayflower visa,
The Hebrews from their Lord's creation
And Indians from annihilation.

Some fancy races like the German
Trace their time from a king called Herman,
While Arabs from Mohammed time deduce,
And Greeks trace themselves right back to Zeus.

It must be lovely for all these tribes
To start from such lofty prototypes,
For none of them would be very wrapped in
Counting their days from a simple Captain.

Buckles, breeches, telescope, book,
We cherish our little Captain Cook.
We love this honest reckless sailor
For running slap into Australia.

Our Good Old Discoverers

We are the only continent with the distinction of having been discovered again and again and again. We don't mind.

We love our discoverers on the ball
Though they're not easy to recall.

We love Perouse for coming too late
And love George Bass for being straight.

We love little Tasman for being able
To bring nice apples to our table.

We love James Cook for his endeavour
And Bill Dampier for his - whatever.

Wentworth we love for crossing blue hurdles
And Flinders we love for going in circles.

We like Leichhardt for being compelling
But Wills we like for his easy spelling.

THE INCREDIBLE HULKS

By 1787 the British Government was running out of room for its prisoners.

For a hundred years or more the Pom
   Deports his convicts overseas
To zones removed and draws therefrom
   A life of luxury and ease.

For a hundred years or more he mails
   His lags to shores American,
Since irrespective of the gaols
   What chains can't do a ferry can.

But selfish Yanks bring things to a halt
   In Boston unsuspectedly,
And dump the Poms like a thunderbolt
   With convicts unexpectedly.

For lack of space, in barge-like hulks
   They're housed with fumes most noxious,
Their numbers swell and Britain sulks
   With their collective conscious.

Crammed and chained on transports hoy,
   Devised by shipwrights bribable,
The outcasts get the chance to enjoy
   Conditions indescribable.

'Where to send them, what can we try?'
   Lord Sydney picks locality,
And indirectly earns, thereby,
   Geographic immortality.

All aboard at Spithead on the south coast of England.

All Aboard

On May 13, 1787, while George Washington was being elected first President of the new American Convention in Philadelphia, in England an equally dramatic event was taking place.

From London sails a fleet of ships
   Of rascals and rascality
In charge a Captain who just drips
   Compassionate humanity.
'Tis Arthur Phillip, kindly sport,
   One thousand pounds per annum net,
By Whitehall hired to help deport
   Their lumpen proletariat.

'Oh, please, deport them all for good,
   Both outcast and felonious,
For English life without them could
   Be charming and harmonious.
Here's five escorts and six jail craft
   To take them across the ocean,
And as the fleet is understaffed
   We'll give you a promotion.'

They give him too with bally-hoo
   Full powers plenipotentiary,
And happy Britain waves goodbye to
   The bobbing penitentiary.
Aboard a gaggle of London folk,
   Who number a thousand and forty-four,
Who do not prize fate's masterstroke
   And rather lack esprit de corps.

The warship *Sirius* leads the fray
   Five hundred tonnes dramatical,
While the *Supply* and *Borrowdale*
   Are a bit less problematical.

With *Charlotte, Friendship, Fishbourne* sails
  The *Scarborough* and *Golden Grove*.
With *Lady Penrhyn* and *Prince of Wales*,
  Goes the *Alexander* painted mauve.

For forty weeks from North to South
  Art steers the fleet with fearlessness,
And never bleak words leave his mouth
  As he reflects their cheerlessness.
Yet Phillip suffers when the lash
  Is plied without causality,
It breaks his heart to see them thrash
  A convict with brutality.

Oh, how he cringes when the screws
  Flog convicts with dexterity
When troubled felons scream abuse
  He writhes in great extremity.
As luck would have it sheer bad nerves
  Make Phillip seek monotony,
So the First Flotilla never swerves
  And heads direct for Botany.

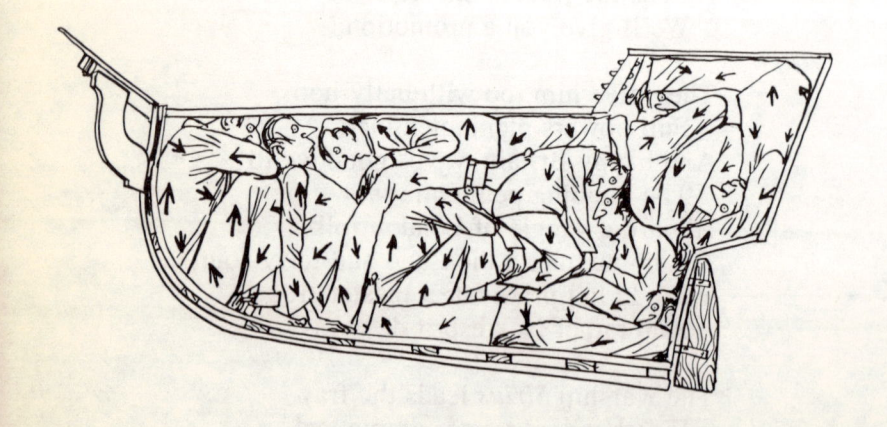

THE FIRST FLEET STATISTICS

1787

Let us now review the facts
And our poor brains not overtax.

Leaving Britain's earthly heaven,
In the First Fleet, ships eleven.

Guided by their Commodore
Sailed settlers a thousand and forty-four.

Chained up on the floating pen
Cursed round about six hundred men.

Fettered and not having too much fun
Lay women one hundred and ninety-one.

Keeping the lid on these captive sardines
Slouched two hundred and six marines.

Now let's not imagine chiefs aplenty,
The figure there was more like twenty.

But to ensure their breed survives
They brought some twenty-seven wives.

Above and below ran thirty kids
Who wouldn't have stayed home for quids.

That's the facts and them's the figures
Of those who faced our early rigours.

16 A Hop Through Australia's History

Australia Day

On 26 January, 1788, while in London Admiral John Byron's grandson, Lord Byron, was coming into the world, another future Admiral of the Fleet, Arthur Phillip, was overseeing a different kind of birth.

Here is a point most pertinent:
How does one claim a continent?

It's an aspect that's most vital
This imperial trick of claiming title.

Phillip certainly was au fait
And thought he'd pick Australia Day.

At dawn he bid some ground be cleared
Of vegetation he found weird.

The lads picked out a likely tree,
Chopped off its grandeur at the knee.

Then stuck it right back in the earth
In readiness for the Nation's birth.

Packing a play-lunch modest but hearty
Phillip threw a flagpole party.

The sky was blue, the weather steamy
The haze on the Cove all sort of dreamy.

No sign of storms, or rain, or thunder -
The perfect day for a little plunder.

Legs unsteady but with esprit
The small group landed at Circular Quay.

They drank a toast, played a drum roll
And hoisted Jacky up the pole.

They played some cricket, then some poker
Though Phillip's game was mediocre.

They drank more toasts, played some bugle
And consumed their picnic frugal.

Then out of earshot up the beach,
Phillip made a laconic speech:

'Testing, testing, one two three
I claim this spot for King and me.

'Testing, testing, four five six
Watch out for those blacks with sticks.

'Testing, testing, eight nine ten,
I think I might do this again.'

Australia Night

The men of the First Fleet came ashore on 26 January, 1788, but it wasn't until 12 days later that the women were permitted to land.

This event is no fancy myth,
We have it first from surgeon Smyth.

He saw the women, saw the men,
And brought us back a specimen.

We also know it from Ralph Clark
Who told them all to disembark.

He watched it from the shrubbery
And jotted in his diary.

Twelve days after hoisting the Jack
Phillip ordered all to unpack.

Dinghies crossed the harbour rip
And took the women off the ship.

When their clothes began to flutter
The feel was like a pound of butter.

When their hair flashed in the sun
The sight was like a pint of rum.

When they alighted at Sydney Cove
The air grew like a heated stove.

When they stepped upon the dry
The ranks of men sighed the deepest sigh.

There huddled puzzled in a band,
The women gazed upon the land.

A tract by now had been axed clean
In the vista eerie green.

The men had worked around the clock
And created a rough campsite block.

Now they stood, their mouths agape
Having forgotten the female shape.

The ground was cleared, the tents were pitched,
The guards guarded, the criminals itched.

Forty weeks cooped up in a galley
And you do not dilly-dally.

On the stormy shoreline, hot and sweating,
Stood the convict women fretting.

On the hushed worksite the men stood tall,
Hanging round for night to fall.

A night of storm winds, panics, rations,
The night First Fleeters loosed their passions.

Unknowing heroes one and all
Now jettisoned class rigmarole.

There was no time for class distinction,
On this, the sharp edge of extinction.

Plunging into a common vortex
Re-wiring the English cortex.

Locked up in a common blood cell
New Australia in a nutshell.

See the crumbling of old order
Warrant seaman ward off warder.

For each one from eight to eighty
Future's grim but pretty matey.

Australia Night

See cavorting drunken capers,
Petties drunk with pretty drapers.

See the waves that lash the harbour,
Phillip's tent beneath the arbour.

Thunder at deafening decibel,
They must have thought themselves in hell.

The ultimate of metaphors:
Welcome kids to the great outdoors.

Thus what today is Macquarie Place,
Saw the birth of a brand new race.

The night of sixth of February,
The night that gave them sanctuary.

A night of chaos and delight,
The very first Australia Night.

THE YEAR OF HUNGER

The small band of emaciated men and women hanging on to the edge of Australia at Sydney Cove in 1790 suffered terrible privations.

Do not imagine
   Once off that ship
Too much stiff
   English upper lip.

In the paintings
   They might look suave
But all the folks did
   In fact was starve.

Two years after
   The Fleet's arrival,
They were struggling
   For plain survival.

This fleet, this band,
   This mass Britannic
Was mostly on
   The edge of panic.

Rags replaced
   Their once fine fashions
And all went round
   On quarter rations.

Some dreamed only
   Of pot roasts,
Following orders
   Like empty ghosts.

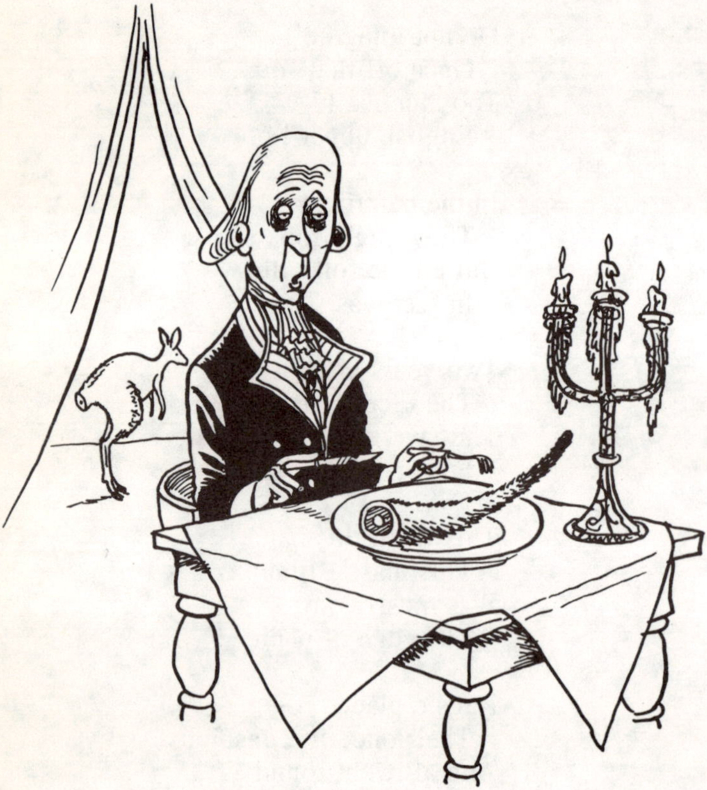

In another the wish
  To be fed was fervent,
Having always been
  A cared-for servant.

A few rebellious
  In the extreme
Could do nothing
  But steal and blaspheme.

Sure they were forgers
  And pocket pickers
But what they were mostly
  Was city slickers.

Londoners usually,
  Urbane and refined
Who found themselves now
  On the edge of mankind.

Picture not a crowd
  Of arrrghing crowers,
These people were
  Regular theatre goers.

The folk made to axe
  The bush in great fear
Once booed and applauded
  Arne and Shakespeare.

The captives now forced
  To harrow and heave
Once ate sherbet and icecream
  During plays by Congreve.

So do not imagine
  Some feral folk
These first Australians
  Came from the big smoke.

Aboriginal Rebels

Around 1800 Aborigines realised that the settlers weren't going to go away and began to resist the white invasion. Their armed struggle was to last more than seventy years.

I'm Pemilwoy
Of Botany Bay,
Hunted by King,
Pickled like prey.

    I'm Mosquito
    A Dharruk hand,
    Hanged by settlers
    For defending my land.

I'm the warrior
Saturday
'Dispersed' at Bathurst,
To 'make way'.

    I was the tribesman
    Mowed without pardon,
    To make Tasmania
    An English garden.

At Binjarra
I bore the noose
So West Australia
Could be all yours.

    I bled to death,
    Hunted and shot,
    You are Australia,
    Because I'm not!

THE CASTLE HILL UPRISING

In 1804 Napoleon's armies had liberated half the nations of Europe, the Irish were convinced that the English were about to fall, and their secret hopes percolated as far as New South Wales.

Convict Johnson, rebel Irish,
At Castle Hill makes speech firish,
Stirs to action his tovarisch,
Sticks and staves and hoes they flourish,
Happy dreams of freedom nourish,
But their plans soon go haywirish,
For among them traitors swinish
The sacred name of mateship tarnish.

Informed Command in speech hellfirish,
Now sets Anglos against Irish,
Routing rebels then proves childish,
And the Irish fate is garish,
Hanged in batches without Kaddish
In great suffering they expirish,
The rest lashings of lashes punish.

The net result of all this bilish,
Wasn't really all that stylish,
Protestants just grew more waspish,
Tried harder in their exiled anguish
Tough Catholics to disestablish.

The 'Rum' Rebellion

Going under various names such as the Royal Marines, New South Wales Army Corps, the Regiment or the Rum Corps, the Police had powers of life and death over everyone. In 1808 it came in direct conflict with Governor Bligh.

Captain Phillip
   Leaves Sydney Cove,
Frank Grose, in charge,
   Says mazel-tov.

U.S.S. "Hope"
   Arrives with liquor,
New South Wales Police
   Turns trafficker.

Hunter comes
   But fails thoroughly,
Officers keep
   The booze monopoly.

Their power King
   Tries to overcome,
Allows ex-convicts
   To sell rum.

But Police hang on
   To their stranglehold,
Succeed in getting
   King recalled.

Famed for toughness
   Bligh is sent
To break up
   the smart Regiment.

Crown-owned rations
  Bligh disburses,
Seizes Rum Corps stills
  And their purses.

Macarthur using
  Tactic rubbery,
Attempts on Bligh
  Some subtle bribery.

Bligh refuses
  What's called barter,
Bids his men:
  'Arrest Macarthur!'

Police officials,
  Guarding their belly,
Promptly counter,
  'Not on your nelly.'

Loyal Rum Corps
  Threaten to retort,
And free Macarthur
  From the Sydney Court.

Major Johnston
  They instigate
Against Bill Bligh
  And his Judge Advocate.

And so the Major,
  In ignoble melée,
Arrests Bill Bligh
  On Australia Day.

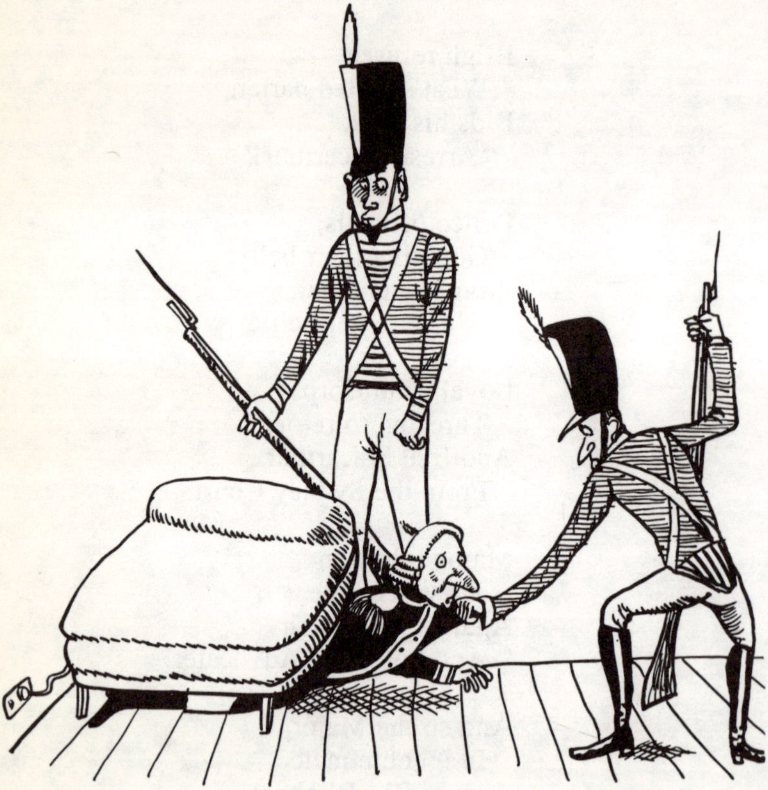

Billy Bligh

William Bligh left Sydney in 1808 after being its Governor for only seventeen months. Born in 1754 he became notorious for the mutiny on the 'Bounty'. He died in England aged 63.

Billy Bligh has gone to sea,
Gone to get the bread fruit tree,
The man just loves to disagree,
   Captain Billy Bligh.

Billy Bligh is lower class,
Disconcerts the *Bounty*'s brass,
Officers give him the arse,
   Ousted Billy Bligh.

Billy Bligh is stern and grim,
By dinghy crosses the big swim,
Gets to London in good trim,
   Stalwart Billy Bligh.

Billy Bligh there has his say,
Lives to be boss another day,
Governor of Botany Bay,
   Successful Billy Bligh.

Billy Bligh grows angry and red
Fights with the Rum Corps instead,
Has to hide under the bed,
   Bad-tempered Billy Bligh.

Governor Bligh leaves in a huff,
But London can't praise him enough,
Which proves it pays one to be tough,
   Admiral Billy Bligh.

Home on the Sheep's Back

Some may remember John Macarthur from the two-dollar bill. In 1817 he returned from exile having been pardoned for his role in the 'Rum' Rebellion against William Bligh. He died in 1834, aged 67.

Young lieutenant
  Joins the Corps,
Arrives in Sydney,
  Stands at the fore,

Hates our wasteland
  Penitential,
In wool growth sees
  Our great potential.

Seizes land,
  Acts like a bully,
Ships from the Cape
  Some Merinos woolly,

Spanish rams crossed
  With Bengal ewes -
'For sheep as meat
  I've got no use.'

Domineering,
  Loud and cruel,
Wounds his Commander
  In a duel.

Sent back to England
  For his excesses,
His fine wool there
  Everyone impresses.

Returns to Sydney
 Undeterred,
Brings more sheep
 From George the Third.

Mocks Bligh's daughter
 Before the gents,
Bligh retorts,
 Pulls down his fence.

Next thing Macarthur
 Will not pay
Fine for a convict
 Stowaway.

Bligh taunts Mac
 With ten of the best,
While Mac initiates
 Bligh's arrest.

Sent to England
 For his rebellion
Our rugged hero
 Proves Machiavellian.

Publicises his
 Ovine fold,
His wool wins honours,
 He wins gold.

The Bigge Report

With Napoleon defeated at Waterloo, reactionary forces felt safe once more to suppress all dissent and opposition. In 1818 they decided to take a good hard look at New South Wales.

Up in London they get queasy
Things Down Under are too easy,
Convict policy is in error
What those buggers need is terror,
Scare in Britain the aberrant
Make Botany Bay a deterrent.

With command to vex and worsen
London sends a polite person
Born of cunning country gentry
The upper class's perfect sentry,
Inspector Bigge arrives on *Barry*
Justice solely to miscarry.

After quick stint of inspection,
Saying things without inflection,
Touring sites from quay to quarry,
Making nervous poor Macquarie,
Bigge reports to his noble friends,
And this is what he recommends:

'Shudder not to be the ogre,
Search hard for the ideal flogger,
Lash'em, kick'em, club'em, flay'em,
Spark off unbearable mayhem,
Keep them down and keep them smitten,
Boys, you're doing this for Britain.'

In the Eighteen Twenties climate
Morale collective starts to plummet,
Bigge's report turns out a scorcher,
Sparks off fiendishness and torture,
Starts to spread unwanted horror
From Newcastle to Illawarra.

Terror Australis

Much of our civilisation today is built not upon the guilt of those early convicts but upon their horrendous and unimaginable pain which increased even more in the 1820's.

On Norfolk Island there's a boss
   His face is like a mask of death,
And everywhere this monster goes
   He leaves behind a mangled mess.
He orders irons to be worn
   Manacles lined with sharpened nails
And men wish they had not been born
   Beneath the fury of his flails.
It's a hundred lashes for a song
   Another hundred for a smile,
The tough get shut in cells oblong
   Locked in darkness and immobile.
Why do they love to lash us so?
   The long tormented convicts cry;
Why, Morisset's everywhere, you know,
   And to that there is no reply.

At Fullerton Cove there is a camp
   Its naked convicts work in chains,
They struggle on the jagged damp
   And undergo horrendous pains.
They toil bare-foot on the shore
   And burn up oyster-shells for lime,
And hump the sacks in choking fear
   A hundred metres through the brine.
With shaven heads and banded necks
   They're flogged each morning for the drill
And irrespective of their sex
   Are ordered back into the swill.
The salty water burns their scars,
   The sacks of lime now drag them down,
'It spares the hangman,' say their guards,
   As they deliberately drown.

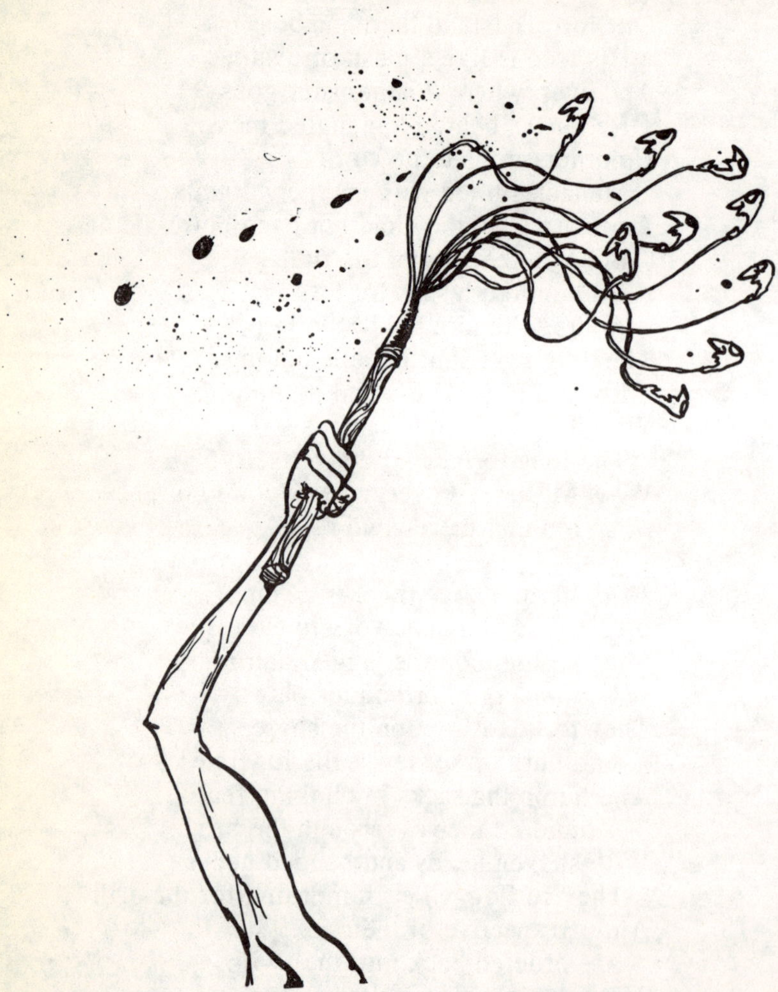

At old King's Town there is a mine,
   Its tortured captives live like brutes
The camp is fostered like a shrine
   To laud the might of British boots.
In shafts no taller than three feet
   The convicts mine for years on end
Supplying coal for Sydney's need
   In irons shackled hard and penned.
The pit is called by all 'Hell's Gate'
   Below Newcastle's early slums,
With miner's flogged at a steady rate
   And to the ready beat of drums.
For twenty tons a day of coal
   Must be clawed out by every shift
And those who do not meet the goal
   Are tied to triangles and whipped.

Where Morisset controls the show
   In full regalia like a czar
A thousand convicts stand in a row
   Compelled to cheer and to hurrah.
The soldier who is deemed to shirk
   The force of blows when giving lash
Himself is placed beneath the birch
   While whipping still the convict trash.
And thus long rows of bloodied backs
   Are seen as normal in that churn
With Morisset astride his nags
   The whipped one whipping in his turn.
In darkness, pains, and heavy odds,
   With taste of death in soul and mouth,
Unfolded thus the fate of Aus,
   In this the Auschwitz of the South.

SHE'LL BE APPLES

Tasmania's third Governor, William Sorell, left the island in 1824, by which time the Colony had grown into an established community. It had taken twenty years of hardship.

Old Mother England
   When she feared the Frogs
Shipped off to Van Diemen's Land
   A batch of underdogs.

They travelled in two ships
   Landed on the Derwent
Where good old Governor Collins
   Led them on most fervent.

For this bunch of settlers,
   We convicts cleared the earth,
In no time whatsoever
   Hobart Town saw birth.

The hardships now increase
   As does the size of gaols,
And all of us are starving
   Till they discover whales.

Just as things improve
   And they get us out of rags
Norfolk Island sends us
   A tough new batch of lags.

Lawlessness grows rife
   Bushrangers wage war
Governor Davey comes and
   Puts us under martial law.

While the Colonial office
  With convict problems grapples,
The Old Hands who get freedom
  Are allowed to grow some apples.

No more ratbags, please,
  Cry us Tasmanian flock,
But still from Britain's gaols
  These tens of thousands dock.

Only one solution,
  The west side of our land
Is turned into a fortress,
  Sorell's by command.

A big sigh of relief
  Stirs through the neighbourhood.
Now steady streams of settlers,
  And apples getting good.

John Batman

As a young man John Batman had already won fame for capturing bushrangers in Tasmania. However in 1835, at the age of thirty-four, he was to gain everlasting glory.

John Batman wished to buy some land
    And took along his riches,
A shirt, a knife, a tomahawk
    A handkerchief with stitches,
A looking glass without a frame
    A few discarded blankets,
A bag of flour and a hundred pounds
    Of most attractive trinkets.

John Batman sailed to Port Phillip Bay
    Upon his chartered schooner,
And when he saw the splendid place
    He wished he had come sooner.
He went to see the countryside,
    Bellarine and Corio,
And exclaimed in great excitement,
    'If there's a seller I'm a buyer!'

John Batman looked round for a chief,
    And frankly told the locals,
'I want to meet the folks in charge
    And not you silly yokels.'
He searched around for days on end,
    With grit from playing rugger,
And didn't stop till he came across
    The brothers Jagajaga.

John Batman he bowed very deep,
    For he could be such a sweetie,
And showed the Jagajaga chiefs
    A most advantageous treaty.

John explained in general terms
   That he had devised a charter,
And was prepared to buy the bay
   By equitable barter.

John Batman was a man of faith,
   Who wished to make things legal,
For he was rather keen to miss
   Any unpleasant sequel.
The chiefs agreed to take a knife,
   So that none will misquote 'em,
And carve in bark most faithfully
   The stamp of their tribal totem.

John Batman then retraced their mark
   Upon the official contract,
Which just explained in simple terms
   The vastness of his land tract.
He now received handfuls of soil
   From the Jagajaga shrewdies,
And in exchange for Melbourne
   Handed over all his goodies.

MYALL CREEK

In 1838, while the colonies prospered economically, human rights left a lot to be desired.

Dreadful is the killing
   The killing of the race
On whose lands we squatted
   Stealing all their space.

It went on for many years,
   Years that deep shame bring,
From Phillip's day of landing
   To Giles of Ullaring.

When the First Fleet landed
   It wasn't very long
Till Kooris became angry,
   Things started to go wrong.

The wrong of greed for acres,
   The principle of grasp,
The odd idea that Kooris
   Just weren't meant to last.

When the tribes resisted
   Rage began to grow,
With every coloniser
   Asserting open go.

When the tribes retorted
   Whites forgot their reason,
Even Governor Brisbane
   Broadcast open season.

Using the excuse of
   One lone farmer speared,

Morisset caused havoc
    Legions disappeared.

Most whites just used weapons,
    The Faithfulls every trick,
Poisoned sheep and water
    Spiked with arsenic.

Under Munn some forty
    Kooris end up shot,
To set them an example,
    Their bodies left to rot.

When Governor Gipps appalled
    Orders speedy peace
Settlers laugh him off,
    Loathsome crimes increase.

Horrid mutilations,
    Whole clans walled in caves,
Warriors dismembered,
    Children used as slaves.

Women forced to wear
    Their husbands' severed heads,
Captured girls imprisoned
    Chained to logs and beds.

The massacre goes on,
    The episodes are bleak,
And reach their ugly climax
    At northern Myall Creek.

Fifty Kooris butchered
    For no specific cause,
Other than that settlers
    Disregard the laws.

Governor Gipps outraged
    Decides to take a stand,
Counter to opinion
    Tries all station hands.

A small child's single rib
  Ends the shameless pantomime,
Against all expectation
  Whites are judged to hang for crime.

One enormous outcry
  Sweeps across the land,
Bigotry unleashes,
  Madcap rescue's planned,

But the Governor is firm
  And seven white men hang,
Kooris are still butchered,
  Now really underhand.

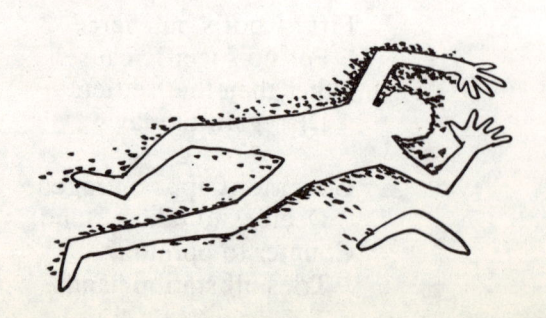

Billy *Charles* Wentworth

By 1840 William Wentworth was one of the big landowner-squatters of the colony. He was fifty years old and would dominate public life for another thirty years.

Wentworth aspires
Descent from squires.
What rude shock -
It's convict stock!

Makes up for blow,
Amasses dough,
Gains wealth woolly,
Acts like bully.

Crosses with class
Blue Mountains pass,
Effects with Sudds
Darling's disgrace.

With news sheet rips
Governor Gipps,
Vast tracts of land
Wants convict manned.

Trial by jury
Is his next fury,
Decrees vital
'Bunyip' title.

Drafts in fusion
Constitution,
To cow the hoards
Wants House of Lords.

Buys South En Zed
From Maori head,
Leads Upper House
Before his bows.

Caroline Chisholm (1808 - 1877)

Caroline Chisholm

In 1841, at the age of thirty-three, Caroline Chisholm obtained permission to open a Female Immigrants' Home in a disused barracks building near Circular Quay in Sydney.

Caroline Chisholm's stance is fearless:
Stop abusing all the sheilas!

Neat in habit, mild in manner,
Like a slumside Pollyanna.

Finds girls day job, gets them shelter,
Won't allow the boss to belt her.

Brings to Outback, before railroads,
Door to door the girls in drayloads.

Female Migrant Home she tenders,
Sixteen branches, inland centres.

Goes to Gipps and sues a doctor
Who once soaked a girl and socked her.

Dogged creature on her own cracked
Proper form of service contract.

Woman's pace of progress quickens,
Models Jellyby for Dickens.

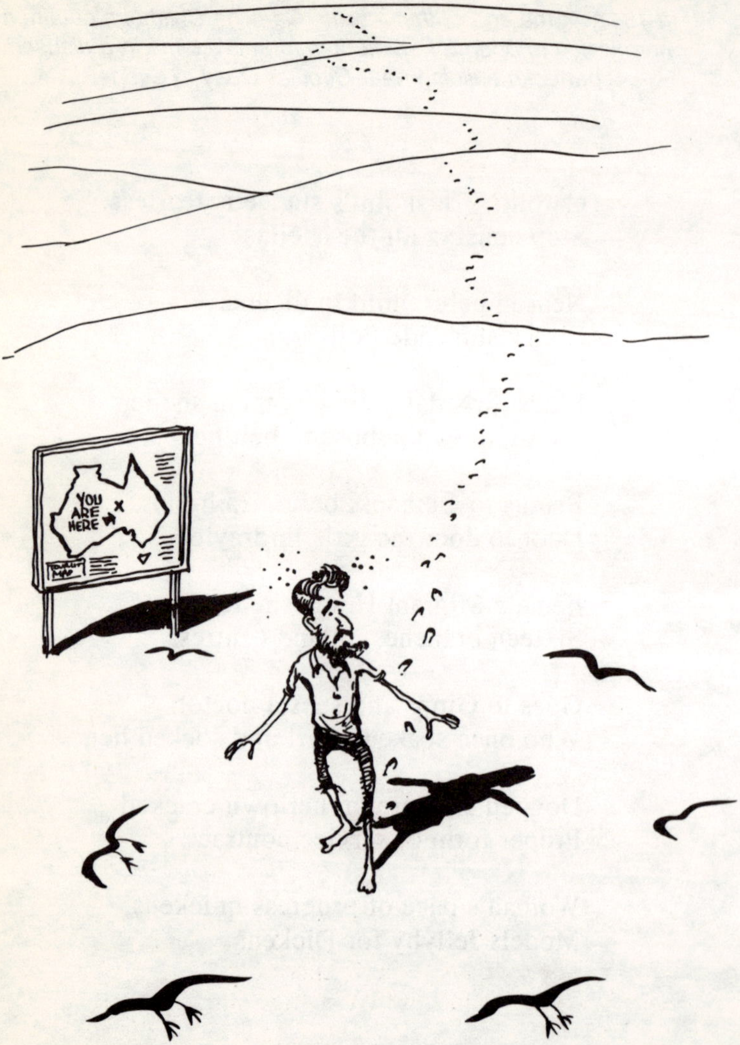
YOU
ARE
HERE

Ludwig Leichhardt

Leichhardt's explorations took place between 1844 - 1848.

Ludwig Leichhardt,
   Gourmet diehard,
Decides to chart
   The North West heart.

After good start
   Plans fall apart,
Taken off guard
   He loses a pard.

Stumbles ill-starred,
   Acts like de Sade,
Pigs out on lard,
   And possum roulade.

After year of hard
   Desert promenade,
Gains the North scarred,
   And is held in regard.

Now avant-garde,
   Honoured in art,
Myopic Leichhardt
   The West wants to chart.

Gathers vanguard,
   While Eyre and Sturt smart,
Leaves much hurrahed
   On new Westward start.

No Bonaparte,
   He finds his way barred,
Dies lost and charred
   In desert graveyard.

Ten Little Governors

The job of being Governor of New South Wales was not a very pleasant one. The last one was appointed in 1846.

Founding the colony makes him sick,
Phillip now resigns in pique.

When the Rum Corps spits in his face,
Hunter goes home in disgrace.

King cannot control rum mania,
So he settles poor Tasmania.

Bligh and the army clash over rum
But the booze rebellion dies in the bum.

Reforms, new towns, convicts, all shine,
Macquarie's still forced to resign.

Lord Brisbane's moods get awful shitty,
He chucks a fit and founds a city.

Dreary Darling rules by decree,
Makes public service convict free.

Bourke polices Port Phillip Bay,
Hands out lands at ten pounds p.a.

Under Gipps the squatters lament,
See the birth of our first parliament.

Under Fitzroy great euphoria,
Goldfields, laws, and Victoria.

Victorian Gold

Everyone started out by moving to New South Wales in 1851 but then, in no time at all, they all moved south to Victoria.

Prospector Hargraves
  With his new technique,
Discovers pay-dirt
  In Bathurst Creek.

Fitzroy's orders
  None will hear,
A hundred thousand
  Flock to Ophir.

People abandon
  Work and home,
Running for digs like
  Gulgong, Turon.

Victoria's farms
  Are empty of men.
Their flight La Trobe
  Is unable to stem.

Melbourne town worries,
  Offers reward,
To those who might find
  Victorian gold.

By some miracle,
  Within four moons
Coach driver Esmonds
  Strikes gold at Clunes.

Grabbing pans, cradles,
  Thingummyjigs,
Huge hordes now swarm
  To Victoria's digs.

THE ADORATION OF THE MINERS

Victorian Gold

Governor La Trobe
   Shows his disgust,
Makes licence fees
   A rigorous must.

It's hopeless to try,
   The gold rush just grows,
The two Colonies
   Metamorphose.

From New South Wales
   The rush goes downstate,
As ticket-of-leave men
   Cross the Bass Strait.

In Heathcote, Bendigo
   And Ballarat,
Voracious diggers
   Are going ratatat.

And miners come from
   All over the world,
The Chartists turn up,
   Their flags unfurled.

The French arrive,
   Swedes, Austrians, Yanks,
Along with phoneys,
   Impostors, cranks.

The Chinese flock too
   And swarm the sites,
Working the mines
   Abandoned by whites.

Australia's invaded
   Without scruples,
Our population
   All but quadruples.

And while folks come here
   Hearts billowing hope,
Australia learns how
   To grow up and cope.

The Eureka Stockade

On 11 November, 1854, miners met and demanded the abolition of the licence system.

Eighteen fifties,
   Ballarat.
Thirty thousand miners,
   Mad.

Licence hunters
   Virulent.
Blame's on Hotham's
   Government.

Chartist rebels
   Stir the crowd.
Peter Lalor's
   Very loud.

Wednesday
   Burn down taverner.
Thursday
   Challenge Governor.

Friday
   In self-defence
Miners build
   A paling fence.

Rebels behind
   Parados
Proudly raise
   The Southern Cross.

Their defence is
   Passionate
Against gun
   And bayonet.

Sunday morning.
   Troops arrive.
Miners murdered.
   Twenty-five.

Hotham Britain
   Won't endorse.
Goldminers
   Become a force.

After some brief
   Punishment,
Rebels join
   Establishment.

Peter Lalor
   Escapee,
Soon enough
   Becomes M.P.

Burke and Wills and Wright and Brahe

The 'Titanic' of Australian inland expeditions set out with a supposedly invincible convoy on 20 August, 1860.

Burke leaves Melbourne with eighteen men,
Horses and camels carry them,
To cross Australia is their aim.

Some quit soon. With problems darned,
Wills is placed second in command,
While Wright with stores gets left behind.

At Coopers Creek Burke waits for Wright.
When he's late, with Wills, uptight,
Burke makes a dash for the Northern Bight.

After two hard months they reach the Gulf.
The return trek proves very tough,
Charlie Grey's light is the first to snuff.

Two months later they're back midway,
Brahe's search party misses by a day,
And they head to Melbourne the wrong way.

Next Wright and Brahe begin to seek
Burke and Wills round Coopers Creek,
Not knowing they'd been there a week.

For they had agreed to use as ark
A tree with 'Dig' carved in the bark
But then forgot to place a new mark.

Another month and Burke and Wills
Return to the Creek broke by their ills,
The heat one then the other kills.

Public sympathy's soon whipped up,
They get buried in a huge hubbub
In time for the very first Melbourne Cup

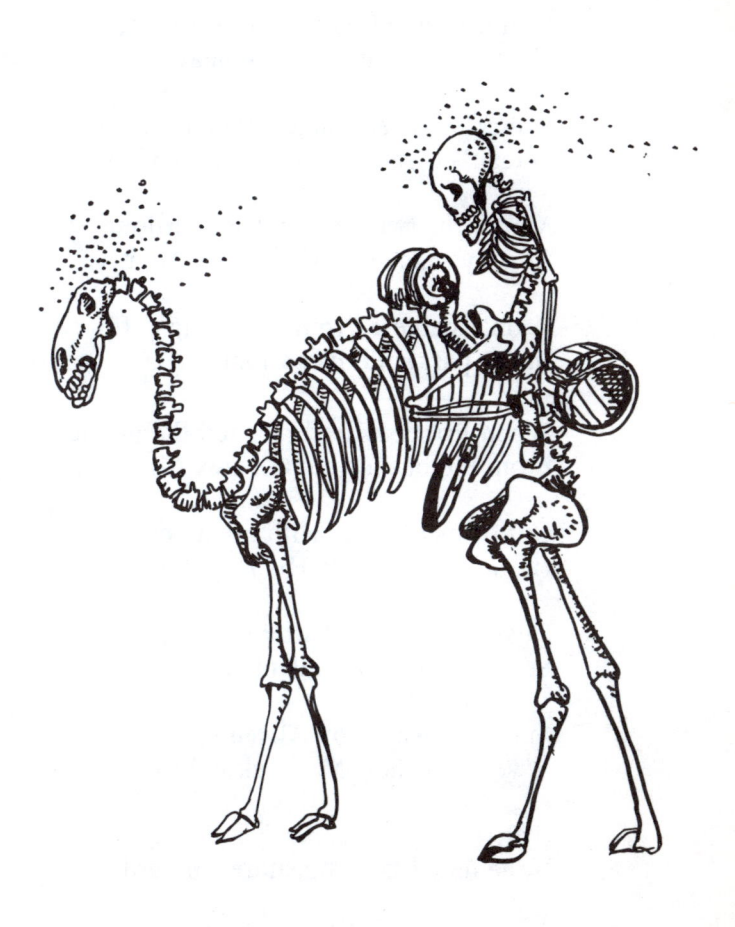

The Royal Visit

Little did Prince Alfred, Duke of Edinburgh, suspect as he landed for the first visit of British Royalty to Australia, the kind of welcome that awaited him in Sydney.

Eighteen hundred and sixty-seven.
Colony thought it was in heaven.

Princely Alfred, duke exquisite,
Queen's own son, sailed in for visit.

March the twelfth saw triple ardour,
Sydney rushed to Middle Harbour.

People gathered round the flagstaff
In the parkland over Clontarf.

When Prince Alfred reached the picnic,
From the bushes burst a sick Mick.

Out of madhouse, with great spryness
He lunged towards His Royal Highness.

Hear a shriek to shatter crystal,
See O'Farrell fire his pistol.

Mark the words by Alfred spoken:
'I've been shot! My back is broken!'

H.R.H. collapses shoreward,
None dare make a gesture forward.

None but one with self-denial,
Coach-builder by the name of Fred Vial.

Pins O'Farrell to the grassy terrain
As he's about to fire again.

Saves the Prince from mortal danger,
Deflects bullet into stranger.

Cops O'Farrell drag to lock up.
Henry Parkes is blamed for cock up.

Alfred wounded to the breastbone,
Shame and chagrin fall like brimstone.

Everyone is shocked and smitten,
'Oh, what will they say in Britain?'

Feeling against the Irish rises,
Plunges Colony in crisis.

WASP and Mick collision rages,
Keeps religion on front pages.

Government gets rather surly,
Alfred gets to leave us early,

Sydney's name gets world-wide blotted
And O'Farrell gets garrotted.

The Man in the Iron Cask

In spite of his imposing and venerable appearance, Ned Kelly was only 25 years-old when he was executed on 11 November, 1880 after a brief but singular career.

Gaoled three years
  For stealing a horse,
When Ned gets out,
  He feels bellicose.

With stepfather George,
  And brother Dan,
He rustles cattle,
  And wears a can.

When Mum gets nicked
  For breaching the peace,
The Kellys attack
  The local police.

They rob a small bank,
  Hold up a wee town,
Then make a last stand
  At Glenrowan.

Holed up in the pub,
  They're captured by ruse,
Gang gets bullet,
  Ned gets the noose.

The case grows famous
  Supporters labour,
Ned Kelly becomes
  A cause celebre.

The message is clear
   For the Poms to heed:
'Britain's convicts
   We no longer need.

'When it comes to
   The criminal clone,
Australia can now
   Produce its own.'

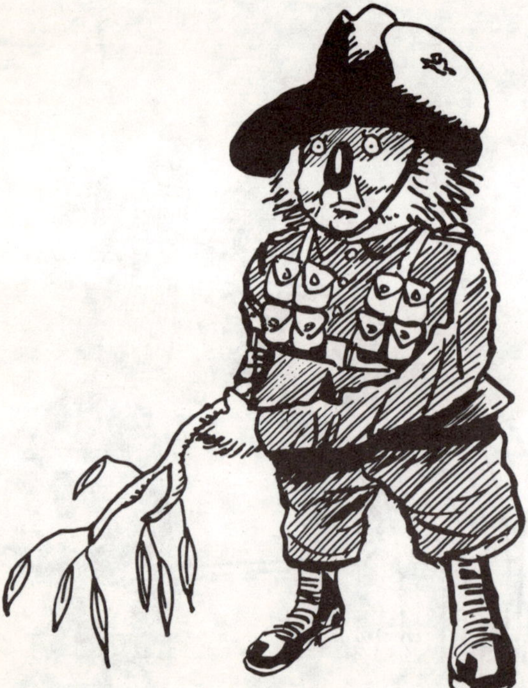

War in the Sudan

*Australia has participated in eight wars,
the first of which was in 1885 in the Sudan.*

The fall of Khartoum
Set Sydney a-boom
With the feverish
Wish
To help refugees
In towns Sudanese
Oppressed
By that pest
The maniacal Mahdi.

In an instant infusion
Of martial effusion
The Colony Premier
A person most linear
Offered to London
Support with abandon
In ammo, resources,
Bronzed Aussies and horses,
Fired,
Inspired
And hardy.

London accepted,
The troops were transepted,
After seagoing larkin'
Got off at Suakin,
Marched on to Tamai
Parched but okay,
Struggled to Digna
In the sunlit enigma
Of the long deserted camelbahn.

The lads fought bravely
With bits of African railway,
Fired dum-dum bullets
Into scrubland pullets,
As they marched
Past locals starving and parched
Trying to connive
How to stay alive,
Amazed at the possies
Of wandering Aussies
Full of gratitude
For being the ones
As those they don't denude
In the struggle and feud
For the sordid burnt barn
That was Britain's Sudan.

On their return,
Four months later they earn,
For fighting the Mahdi's tyranny,
A hero's welcome from the Colony:
People rush from their beds
To see them sail through the Heads,
To see the fresh-faced cherub
Aboard the H.M.S. *Arab*,
Everyone wanted the 'Walers',
Shops were shut by retailers,
Bells were tolled,
Kids were bold,
And with medals pinned on thorax
Long speeches at the Barracks
Celebrate for evermore,
Australia's first taste of war.

The Great Maritime Strike

Unions as we know them today began to appear around 1890. Trouble broke out when owners of shipping lines started to employ Asian labour.

Marine officers want more pay,
Decide to form the M.O.A.
Upset employers ballyhoo,
Get together, form F.E.U.

The Trades Hall Council shouts cooee,
The M.O.A. joins the T.H.C.
The F.E.U. angered, very,
Locks the M.O.A. off ship and ferry.

Exploited shearers' A.S.U.,
Oppressed miners' A.M.A. too,
Decide to aid the M.O.A.
And throw F.E.U. into disarray.

The F.E.U. now tries to destroy
The A.M.A.'s case but gets no joy.
Emboldened by T.H.C. cash,
Soon M.O.A. and F.E.U. clash.

Test case! Test case! A.M.A. strike,
A.S.U. join in, sportsmanlike.
Scared F.E.U. calls P.A.C.,
While Unions form a Defence Committee.

A.M.A. mad declares coal black,
F.E.U. sees no turning back.
A.S.U. arms, sheep go berserk,
Fifty thousand refuse to work.

Supporters mass, country divides,
Vic. and N.S.W. take sides.
The Riot Act's read at Circular Quay,
And employer wins over employee.

The Crash of the 1890's

Keen to keep on sitting pretty
Banks lend without security,
But when in London Westgarth fails,
Aussie stocks take a dive in sales.

When Argentinian banks go bust,
All think Australia also must.
Wool falls, wheat falls, metals plunge,
Aussie banks can no more scunge.

A quarter billion pounds in red,
The Government tries raising bread.
The more it borrows, the more it owes,
So public projects have to close.

Unemployment becomes normal,
Housing mortgages informal,
Bank investors all turn vile,
First bank to flop is Mercantile.

Twelve more banks in ninety-three
Slam their doors in Melbourne's spree.
Having loaned out their funds slapdash
Some forty Credit Unions crash.

With bids to stem the panic hexed,
Eleven more banks plummet next.
With stocks and shares turned into pulp
All Australia can do is gulp.

The moral? If it's familiar cast
It's 'cause banks don't learn from the past,
And though some still play the great temptress,
You're better off with a good mattress.

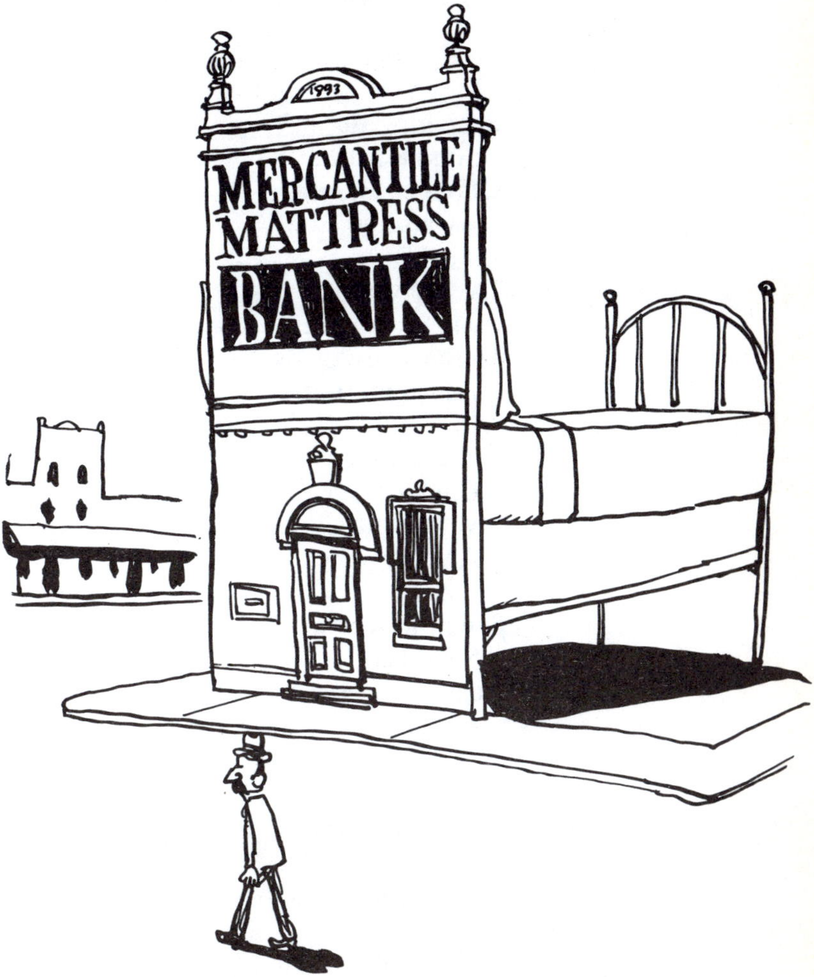
1893
MERCANTILE
MATTRESS
BANK

Lawrence Hargrave

*You know him from the back of the twenty-dollar bill.
Tucked away in Stanwell Park, Lawrence Hargrave
performed an astonishing feat in 1894.*

Searching for an
 Aussie battler?
Laurence Hargrave,
 Aviator.

Twenty years of
 True devotion
To the study of
 Aerial motion.

Our aviation's
 Cinderella
Invents both glider
 And propeller.

See him treat with
 Supercool
Australia's cruel
 Ridicule.

For everybody
 Thinks he skites
When he raves
 About his kites.

Folks look on him
 With irritation
For trying to rise
 Above his station.

But tying four box kites
   Together
Lawrence just waits for
   Bad weather,

Then soars Prometheus-like
   Unbound
A whole five metres
   Off the ground.

Rose Scott pioneered much of the early sufragette movement.

Women Fight for the Vote

In 1894 Australian women found themselves at the forefront of the sufragette movement.

By eighteen eighty drunkenness
   Had become all epidemic,
The issue of male self-control
   Was now purely academic.

Some women thought the only way
   To stop degeneration
Was to bung men in their place
   And cease their veneration.

They wanted females to have the vote
   To ban the sale of liquor,
And undertook a loud campaign
   Australia to transfigure.

The Women's Temperance Union
   As was their designation
Was received both with approval
   And with moral indignation.

'Do no trust them, it's a trick!'
   Cried some housewives with suspicion,
They were the ones who knew that men
   Took delight in their condition.

But there were those who thought it good,
   The Women's League of Suffrage,
Reformer Rose Scott in the lead,
   Cared not if men took umbrage.

The fight soon spread to all the States,
  Where seen by politicians,
As means to increase the number of votes
  Against determined Oppositions.

But it was not till one hot night
  In eighteen hundred and ninety-four,
That in Adelaide's Parliament
  The legislation hit the floor.

The opposition counting numbers even
  An old man suddenly came afore,
And thus the act conferring women
  The right to vote became the law.

Ten years more it took the right
  To vote to spread across the land,
And even then no one believed
  That any woman would want to stand.

So it was not for twenty years
  That a woman won a ballot,
The one who did was Edith Cowan,
  A truly Western Australian zealot.

It then took another twenty,
  And a World War full of terror,
To elect the great Enid Lyons
  To a rep seat in Canberra.

What a concept! What an idea!
  What does one do? Despair? Lament?
Forty years to place a woman
  In the Federal Parliament!

WE'RE OFF TO KILL THE BOERS

When the Boers of South Africa refused to give their British residents the vote in 1899, the Empire declared war on them. Australia was more than enthusiastic in her support.

At the time of Federation
And Empire adoration
Australia agreed
To give a thorough nosebleed
To that awfully cocksure
South African Boer
For denying the vote
To Pommies remote
In some distant kraal
And revenge the loss of Natal.

Men volunteered,
Women donned beards,
Australia feasted,
The A1 enlisted,
The troops once embarked
Another spree sparked,
The waving,
The braving,
The self-celebrating
Simply knew no sating
As sixteen thousand left for Transvaal.

With horsewhip
And grip
On Africa's tip
The Aussie cooee
Was split into three
And they determined advance
Pleased with the chance

To teach the Afrikaners
A lesson in manners
They'd never ever forget.

So there's no dodder
Along the Modder,
No wasted erg
At Pandenburg,
No nit pickin'
At Mafeking,
Just the fair thickset
Determined sweat
Of the keen Australian epaulet
Feeling a wee bit conned
For the enemy's also blond
A lot in fact like ourselves.

Dr Quick

In 1901 Australia became a Federation. One of the people who made this possible was John Quick, a doctor of law who lived from 1852 to 1932.

Doctor Quick of Bendigo
Had the kind of bent ego
And the sort of reputation
That enabled Federation.

Sweet of temper and demeanour
He lured down to Riverina
After months of hot intrigues
All the interested Leagues.

Bigwigs, ratbags, all were present
Locked in bouts of blues incessant
But Quick he found some dinkum ears
And got on side two Premiers.

Then in a speech most passionate
Quick expressed their ideas inchoate,
And releasing pent up tension
Proposed a great convention.

A conference miscellany
Elected in each colony,
Candidates who'll work in fusion
On a brand new Constitution.

Clamour, cheers and shouts of bravo
Welcomed Quick the entire arvo,
All Corowa was in symbiosis
With the doctor's diagnosis.

Dr Quick

In 1901 Australia became a Federation. One of the people who made this possible was John Quick, a doctor of law who lived from 1852 to 1932.

Doctor Quick of Bendigo
Had the idea of federation
And the good reputation
That ended in Federation.

Sweated, raged, and damnation
He liked down with frustration.
Other builders of his might
Lit the passionate fires.

The Quick successor of nations
Lot of colours of blue successes
John Quick the handsome draftsman
Of not on side two Frontiers.

The Quick succeed to those inside
Cheered the their Federal friends,
And cheering all Bendigo
Itemised Great corruption.

A combination discipliary
Electors' eager duty
And cheer will work in fusion
Of a new Constitution.

Chamber, blest and good of grey
Welcomed Quick the softly are,
All Quick to war in cabinets
With the four Yelling brief.

What do you think, Doctor? Any hope?

Dr Quick

For his motion was not random,
The Leagues feared a referendum,
Feared that people in every state
Might not want to incorporate.

And since on every occasion
Votes were few for Federation,
All agreed it was a lot smarter
To get folks to vote for a Charter.

Hearken this, oh anxious public,
All who wish a new republic,
If you want to learn the trick
Then better go to Dr Quick.

Mabel Was I Ere I Saw Melba

Melba's father, David Mitchell, was one of the richest men in Victoria. Inheriting his determination, she became England's foremost soprano. By 1910 her recordings brought her universal fame.

Lovely looking and a Taurus
Might have spent her life in the chorus,
But her Daddy David was a magnate
Who didn't think that one should stagnate.

Firmly like a march by Sousa
She decided her husband was a loser,
And sought Mr Cecchi when she heard he
Could teach the art of singing Verdi.

Her next lessons she took in Paris,
Madame Marchesi was a menace,
But ended being Nellie's helper,
Taught her stardom, called her Melba.

Her true career began in Brussels
Where her voice first showed its muscles,
And when she sang Puccini's Mimi
They could just about hear her in Tarranginnie.

Because her dad was St Patrick's builder
It taught her to reach new heights as Gilda,
And, though unsuited, she saw no harm in
Trying her chords at the role of Carmen.

London next was a lot of fun
For here from eighty-eight till World War One
When her timbre began to harden
She warbled each season at Covent Garden.

She sang also like a great virago
At the Grand Opera in Chicago,
While in New York it was no sweat
To perform Gounod's Juliette.

For years you couldn't find anything purer
Than her corrugated coloratura,
That's why in the Great War, us to inspire,
They made her a Dame of the British Empire.

*Dame Nellie Melba nee Helen Mitchell Armstrong
(1861 - 1931)*

Gallipoli

1915

World War One,
   Turkish front,
Aussie troops must
   Bear the brunt.

Landing missed,
   Wrong cliff climbed,
Birdwood's plans
   Are badly timed.

Allies err,
   Don't fight at once,
Turks bluff all
   With their fake guns.

At Anzac Cove,
   Ground is held,
Trenches dug,
   Turks repelled.

Three weeks later,
   Huge assault,
Combat close,
   But no result.

Next at Nek,
   Then Lone Pine,
Three more thousand
   Find their shrine.

Eight months long
  Aussies tossed,
Gallipoli
  Ends up lost.

Back at home,
  Big hopes thwarted,
The deaths, the deeds
  Become distorted.

Politicians
  Of all description
Fight on the issue
  Of conscription.

Mannix and
  The Left deplore
Our involvement
  In the war.

Hughes with savagery
  And galumph,
Argues that defeat
  Was a triumph.

Australian politics
  Becomes unstable,
Gallipoli becomes
  A fable.

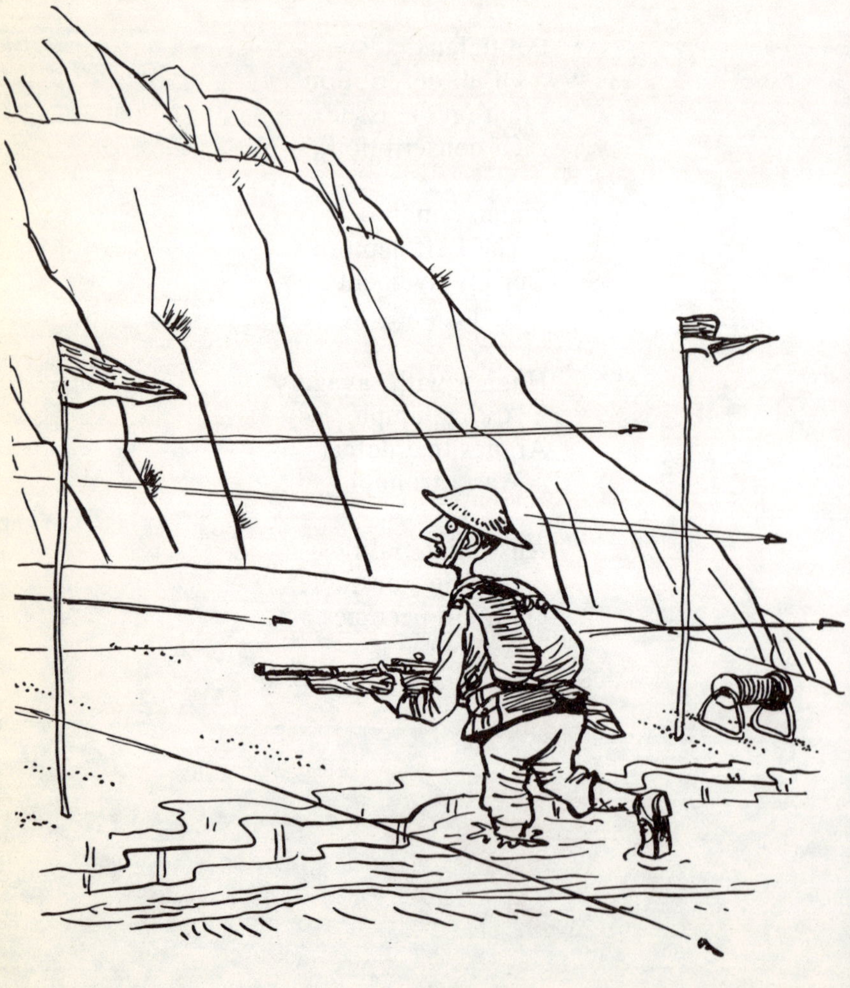

So told me Mrs Dunn

In 1915 the Australian public knew nothing of the battles raging in Turkey. By the time they heard of them, the Allied forces had abandoned the campaign.

There was a dreadful battle
　So told me Mrs Dunn,
She had it from a neighbour
　Who heard it from her son.
The battle was in Turkey
　An awful bad defeat,
Lots of our boys were lost there
　Beating a fast retreat.

'I hate talk of these things, dear,
　Gives me a heavy heart,
But reading last night's Daily
　I saw a little chart.
It clearly showed the places
　From where escaped our boys,
You could see from all the arrows
　That they just had no choice.'

But then old Jim O'Connor
　Our federal MP,
Sent us all a letter saying
　None of them tried to flee.
It was just a vicious rumour,
　Spread by enemy spies:
'It was all a glorious battle,
　And our boys deserve a prize.'

Then there was Mrs Angus,
　I met her at the shop,
Her boy was blown to pieces
　But she didn't mind a jot.

Dave died a glorious hero,
  Just like all the rest,
The Brits they might've mucked things up
  But our boys did their best.

They might have abandoned Lone Pine
  They might have stuffed the Nek,
They might have messed up Suvla
  And their guns let go to wreck,
They might have not got somewhere
  Might not have reached their goal,
They might have lost the battle,
  But I know they gave their all.

Then the Reverend Bill Lawton,
  He's known me since my birth,
Told us that the British Empire
  Was God's Kingdom here on Earth.
The Reverend added slowly,
  For some are none too bright,
That the Anzacs are all heroes,
  And Britain's always right.

On a poster pasted near us,
  Was a speech by Mr Hughes,
Since Aussies are born heroes,
  He believes there's no excuse
To shirk the Empire's battles,
  The Empire is our shrine,
And everyone must conquer
  Like the Anzacs at Lone Pine.

But as I say, this battle,
  Of which told me Mrs Dunn,
Who had it from a neighbour,
  Who heard it from her son,
This battle was in Turkey
  A glorious noble fight,
And our boys turned into men there,
  And proved our nation's might.

POOR HENRY

Australia's favourite writer, Henry Lawson was born on 17 June, 1867 on the goldfields of New South Wales. His father, Neils Larsen, was a Nowegian sailor. His mother, Louisa, after many struggles, started her own magazine, **Dawn**, *dedicated to progressive issues.*

Daddy Lawson, heavy drinker,
   Mummy Lawson, self-obsessed
Little Henry, hard of hearing,
   For some reason feels depressed.

Body fragile, make-up sickly,
   Schooling scanty, loves to write,
Goes to Sydney from the goldfields,
   Harry's in for a rough ride.

Earning wages almost zero,
   He is forced to live in slums,
Deafness cleaves him from society
   It's create or twiddle thumbs.

Too rebellious to join parties,
   Much too touchy to compete,
Age of twenty finds him angry,
   Scribbles 'Faces In The Street.'

Early glory in the papers,
   Poems read in town and bush,
Hits on mates for yarns and drinking
   In a group called 'Mountain Push.'

Workers, unions, social causes,
   Other themes are tramps and swags,
Moves to Albany and Brisbane,
   Where he works on local rags.

Dislikes Asians, blacks not fond of,
　　Thinks the capital system bunk,
Henry's into Truth and also into
　　All the joys of getting drunk.

Alcohol becomes important
　　Breaks the silence, finds him voice,
Not that life in th'Eighteen Nineties
　　Gave a body too much choice.

Body sickly, make-up fragile,
　　Starts to drink at first by stealth,
Goes to Enzed, works a sawmill,
　　Really perfect for the health.

Back in Sydney lives with mother,
　　Who just puts the mockers on,
Knocks up stories about *'Arvie*,
　　Battles Banjo Patterson.

In a bookshop chats up Bertha,
　　Love like art increases thirst,
Harry now goes on a blinder,
　　Writing, writing like one curst.

Drover, stockman, shearer, rider,
　　Barmaid, hooker, farmer's wife,
People stories he produces
　　As if carved with his pen-knife.

Publication brings him stardom,
　　He begs Bertha to be his bride,
Mates want him to write another
　　In The Days When The World Was Wide.

After years of fighting deafness,
　　Finding love just feels so good,
Henry's sick of isolation,
　　Sick of being misunderstood.

Weds young Bertha, sails to West coast,
  Henry's drinking just gets worse,
Works himself into a frenzy
  Then writes militaristic verse.

When their money vaporises
  And the West's slums get them down,
Once more he returns to Sydney,
  Publication and renown.

It's his book of best short stories,
  The result of troubled oils,
One for which he's best remembered,
  Flashbacks *While The Billy Boils*.

But success makes Henry thirsty
  Just as failure did before,
He goes on another bender,
  Getting screwed up all the more.

Hiding from the wary Bertha,
  Drinks but tries not to get caught,
She thinks travel might just help him,
  'Let's go to New Zealand, sport.'

Teaches Maoris on South Island,
  With anxiety goes out of mind,
While his wife's expecting Jimmy,
  Henry's drinking himself blind.

Once again returns to Sydney,
  Once again success in books,
And this time to vary drinking,
  Henry's lured by a woman's looks.

Once again it's time to travel,
  Lawsons three set out at once,
Sights are set this time on London
  And on the State Governor's punts.

Liked in London, works successful,
   Sudden fortune makes him drink,
Hates the English, needs the sunshine,
   Pushes wife to nervous brink.

Nineteen oh three back in Sydney,
   Bertha, Henry, get divorce,
Life is now just boarding houses,
   Drinking, poetry, remorse.

Beethoven, Smetana, Goya,
   Lived identical deaf hell,
Loved mankind but hated people,
   Letting go themselves as well.

We've all seen him on the money,
   Thick moustache, eyes discontent,
Fancy making him a symbol,
   He who never had a cent.

Sure he wrote still, times changed also,
   Roaring twenties wanted fun,
Who had time for social conscience?
   Henry Lawson's days were done.

Folks avoid him Friday morning
   Hope he doesn't come too near,
But by Monday at his burial
   They throng to get close to his bier

Died a pauper and neglected,
   Like the tramps who were his mate,
With some irony, however,
   He scored a funeral of state.

Charles Kingsford Smith Flies Across the Pacific

Born in Brisbane in 1897, he joined the Royal Flying Corps in World War One and fought as a pilot in France. With a strong ambition to become a 'trail blazing' aviator, he set about in 1928 to be the first person to fly across the Pacific.

Smithy the Pilot
   The man of no fuss
Flew up to Heaven
   In his Old Bus.

Once up in Heaven
   What a tableau!
There was the U.S. coast
   Fading below.

Crossing the ocean
   He headed south west
Three Fokker motors
   Roaring with zest.

Charles flew to Hawaii,
   Flew to Fiji
Reaching Australia
   To one huge cooee.

Oakland to Sydney
   Had Smithy traversed,
In eighty-three hours,
   An absolute first.

The Sydney Harbour Bridge

Completed in 1932, it took nine years to build and was financed by a loan from the Rothschild Bank that took over fifty years to pay off.

Harbour Bridge is half kay long
Half kay long, half kay long
Harbour Bridge is half kay long
And is the bridge that Jack built.

Harbour Bridge is fifty wide
Fifty wide, fifty wide
Harbour Bridge is fifty wide
And see the Captain cross it.

Harbour Bridge one thirty tall
One thirty tall, one thirty tall
Harbour Bridge one thirty tall
And good old Bradfield raised it.

Jack and the Lions

Dramatis Personae:
Jack Lang, Premier of New South Wales;
Joe Lyons, Prime Minister of Australia;
Sir Phillip Game, State Governor.
The Place: Sydney. The time: 1932.

Jack Lang
Had a prang
Didn't want to pay the English bank.

Joe Lyons roared
Eyed Jack's hoard
Took no time to pull the cord.

Jack got heavy
Raised a levy
Punched the rich in the underbelly.

Joe Lyons shrill
Ran through a bill
Threw Jack's new tax on the dunghill.

Jack aflame
Staked his claim
But the Governor was tough and Game.

Joe Lyons charged
Game Jack discharged
Everybody marched and countermarched.

Jack Lang sacked
Didn't react
Called it illegal but suffered the fact.

Joe Lyons purred
Aussies concurred
And Jack turned into a mockingbird.

Phar Lap: The Phacts

*The year 1932 saw the completion of the
Sydney Harbour Bridge. It also saw the death of our
most idolised racehorse.*

By Night Raid out of Entreaty,
　His colour was sort of bay,
He was bought by Harry Telford
　Who had hoped to make him pay.
His first four starts - disastrous
　As were also his next three,
And not till a race at Warwick Farm
　Did he invite scrutiny.

Favourite at Rosehill Racecourse
　There he won his first,
At Randwick chopped all his opponents
　Into tiny liverwurst.
Won the Craven Plate by four lengths
　Like no other quadruped,
While in the VRC Derby
　He just left the field for dead.

With four wins under his mane,
　And tipped for the Melbourne Cup,
He got saddled at seven stone six
　But just couldn't get it up.
There followed a spate of losses,
　As well the St George Stakes,
But then in the Autumn season
　He finally broke the hex.

With eight straight wins in three cities
　Phar Lap lay them in the aisles,
And set an Australian record
　For two and a quarter miles.

His jockey was Jimmy Pike,
  Who seldom intervened,
And left tactical decisions
  To the bay-hued 'wunderkind.'

Big Red was now a champion,
  A Tall Poppy, so to speak.
On Derby Day at Flemington
  He even got shot at in the street.
Tommy Woodcock, his brave strapper,
  Jammed him against a fence,
Screened him with his body and saved him
  From racing's malcontents.

It was now time for the greatest race,
  First Tuesday in November,
Phar Lap, the small punter's bastion,
  Hero of every non-member,
Had his odds reduced by bookies
  To a slim eleven to eight,
The shortest priced race favourite
  In the Cup's distinguished slate.

When the day at long last arrived,
  To Aussie days the mother,
The seventieth Melbourne Cup,
  An instant like no other.
Eighty thousand in attendance
  Saw the great Phar Lap perform,
Pass Second Wind then Shadow King
  And amble easily home.

But still it was not quite enough
  For at that very meet
The great bay tore around twice more
  For his triumphal sweep.
It was all part of fourteen wins'
  Uninterrupted breeze,
But then, let's face it, Phar Lap's name
  Means 'Lightning' in Sinhalese.

The horse was now at the apex
  Of his maturity,
And raced the greatest of his life
  In the famed Futurity.
Ten stone three, the weight he carried,
  But awesome his technique,
For still he won in a wondrous burst
  By a neck from Mystic Peak.

But dark forces in the background
  Conspired against Phar Lap,
For the 'tallest poppy' of all time
  Was the subject of much clap-trap,
Men criminal and respected,
  But specially men hard-boiled,
Saw the gelding as a hiccup
  In the running of games well-oiled.

The grand Victorian Racing Club
  Introduced a special fix,
So that for the C. M. Lloyd Stakes
  Phar Lap bore a ton of bricks.
And though he lost that unfair race,
  He fought like billyo,
And still he beat them, still he won
  The next six in a row.

But he kindled hatred and jealousy
  In direct ratio with his size,
The Melbourne Cup of thirty-one
  Proved the start of his demise.
Ten stone ten pounds handicapped
  His load was a disgrace,
And Jimmy Pike just pulled him back,
  Let him chug into eighth place.

It was clear he'd never be allowed
  To prevail in Oz again,
And so his owners devised a plan
  To maximise their gain.

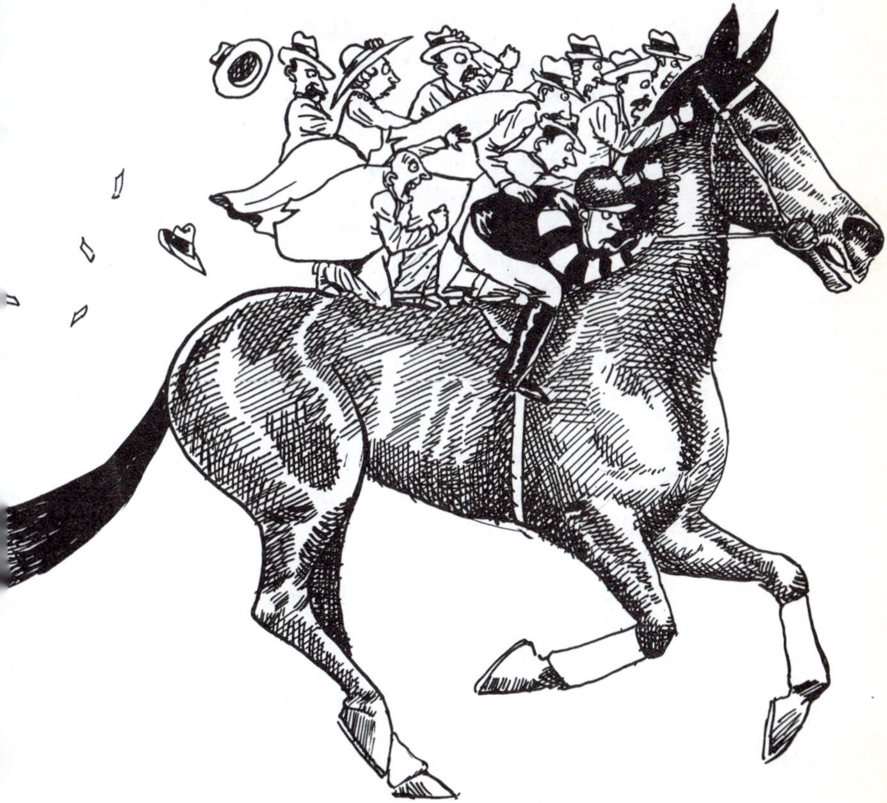

Greed thus ate even deeper
  Into the fate of the great bay,
For his masters shipped him off next
  To Agua Calient-ay.

'The Red Terror from Down Under'
  Set records in New Mexico
And left amazed all those who watched
  And wondered just what makes-him-go.
The Yankees cheered ten furlong's worth
  They loved his loping stride,
And Phar Lap made Australia proud,
  Young Woodcock by his side.

How imposing was his splendour,
  All the Yanks watched him aghast,
How lucky they were to see the race
  For it was his very last.
Munching weeds at Menco Park,
  Two weeks later, on April five,
After a brief sweat and tremor
  Phar Lap was no more alive.

How did it pass? How could it be?
  Was it fortune? Was it caused?
A monster fifteen pounder
  Was all his chest disclosed.
A great heart and a good physique
  That fought to the last crumb,
His spirit is in the people,
  The rest in a museum.

Donald Bradman

Bradman captained the Australian Cricket Team for the first time in 1936. By then he was the world's most famous cricketer. He was only 28 years old.

Donald Bradman, raised in Bowral,
Batting golf-balls felt arousal,
Other kids caroused and grooved,
But Donald hit whatever moved.

While his mates just played the field,
Donald played in Sheffield Shield,
One one eight for a debut
Is not a score you can pooh-pooh.

Don impressed the cognoscenti
Who picked him for a Test at twenty,
Don outshone resentful chums
With sixteen hundred and ninety runs.

He went to England at twenty-two
His score there was uncanny too,
The English flocked to see him bat,
Team mates wished he'd just go splat.

But Bradman's scores kept getting higher,
For he was the Test Messiah
Who, without batting his eye lashes,
Redeemed Australia with the Ashes.

Crowding round the radio receiver
The world was seized by Bradman fever,
In the loungeroom or front porch
Rivalling Churchill and King George.

Don struck the fear of God in Brits
Who underhand devised a blitz,
By aiming bouncers to the crotch
Hoping thus to see him splotch.

But though it plainly wasn't cricket
Donald managed to guard his wicket,
And survived their 'bodyline'
And all that British pantomime.

But Don dreamt of being mediocre,
So moved on to be a stockbroker,
When forced to admit he was supreme
He returned to captain the Aussie team.

From Thirty-six to Thirty-eight
He led the squad to vindicate
The earlier Australian pride
While crowds Donald deified.

Bradman enthralled the Pommy hordes
Batting record scores at Lord's,
Canberra was so delighted
It recommended Don be knighted.

Pig Iron Bob

Robert Menzies, born in 1894 and became Prime Minister for the first time in 1939. Pig Iron Bob was one of his many nicknames and he acquired it when approving the sale of potential war materials to the Japanese.

    Pig Iron Bob
      Come play and skirl
    The Hun is in Warsaw
      The Jap's at the Pearl.

    But where are the men
      Who made on the deal?
    They're in Geneva
      Re-selling the steel.

The Bombing of the North

On 19 February, 1942, two and a half years after the start of the Second World War, Australia's territorial inviolability came to an abrupt end.

Eighty planes from Hirohito
Flew to Darwin incognito.

On a sleepy summer morning
The Japs zapped without warning.

Planes were smashed still on the ground,
Their two main aims: destroy, confound.

Darwin was hit all the harder,
Fifty ships packed the big Harbour.

No dogfight this, no honest Western,
First to go down was the *William Preston*.

The toll was heavy, eight vessels sunk,
Twenty three planes turned to junk.

Many perished as the docks exploded
Even before the guns got loaded.

Two hundred and fifty people died,
And the whole of Australia lost her pride.

The bombing caused a type of panic
Not often seen in folks Britannic.

Terrified of all things Asian
Everyone thought it an invasion.

The Bombing of the North

Yet this was just the start of tricks,
The North copped air raids fifty-six.

Queensland emptied its coastal cities,
The nation got the heebie-jeebies.

Forsworn by Britain to its own fate
Australia felt like a featherweight.

But the country rose from its despair
When America's Kittyhawks took to air.

Closing one of our most traumatic chapters
With big brother's Interceptors.

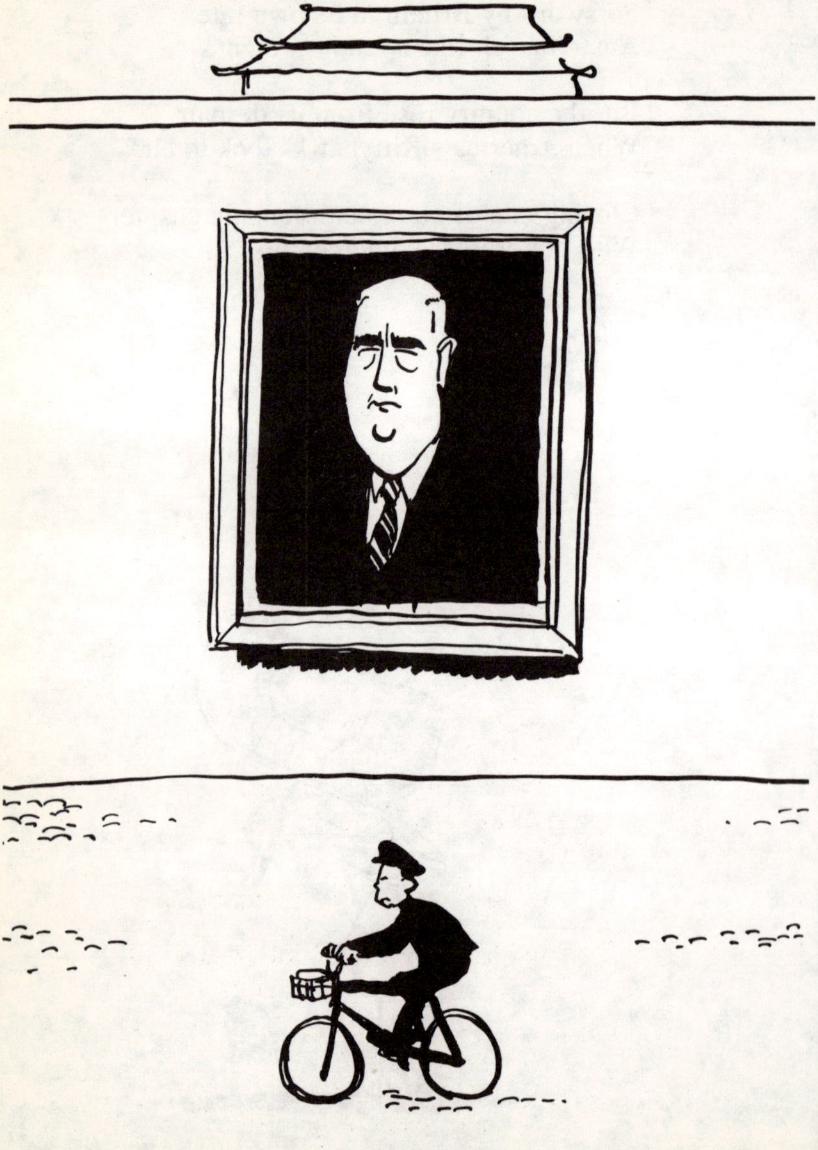

MING

Robert Menzies became Prime Minister for the second time on 10 December, 1949, ten days before his fifty-fifth birthday.

Menzies was a Scotsman,
   Menzies was a brain,
Menzies came to power
   And never left again.

Menzies was a lawyer,
   Wordwise he was deft,
Failed to ban the Commies
   But got to split the Left.

Menzies loved his country,
   Menzies loved his Queen,
The middle classes loved him
   And always got him in.

Menzies formed a party
   At **Albury** made speech,
Promised all a backyard
   And a Hills Hoist each.

Menzies was a fierce man,
   Not someone to chafe,
Migrants all loved Menzies,
   He made them all feel safe.

Menzies was a Scotsman,
   Menzies was a brain,
Menzies came to power
   And never left again.

Thomas Austin, Jean McNamara & The Hundred Year War

1859-1951

Thomas Austin of Geelong
Has a feeling he doesn't belong.

The man is lonely, hates his farm
The place seems empty, without charm.

Thomas Austin gets quite rabid -
What this country needs is rabbit.

Sits at desk, pulls out equipment,
Writes to England for a shipment.

The year is eighteen fifty-nine.
Rabbits arrive in ten months time.

No sooner do they disembark
They run berserk in Barwon Park.

See them hopping, leaping, jumping,
Their lovable back feet thumping.

See them sniffing, whiffing, scouting,
Their furry fluffy cuteness flouting.

Thomas Austin writes wholesaler,
Rabbits really love Australia.

But in the morning when he wakes,
Oh the horror that awaits!

The much prized and treasured star pet
Has turned into a living carpet.

Thomas Austin, Jean McNamara & the Hundred Year War 105

See them digging, jumping, hurdling,
With their pip-squeak squeals bloodcurdling.

'Oh my god,' says Thomas Austin
'This here damage don't bear costin'!'

Thomas winces as he hunts
Shooting rabbits ten at once.

But things soon get a bit too rough,
For he's not shooting fast enough.

Come the neighbours with their shotguns
On the trail of the little hot ones.

Kicking, shooting, punching, shoving
But the beasts not overcoming.

Rabbits in complete euphoria,
Chomping their way through Victoria.

Nothing's sweet or cute or funny
When it comes to Austin's bunny.

Over hillocks, under fences,
The countryside has no defences.

The land becomes a barren floor
All the way to the Nullarbor.

Nothing green has a shred of chance
From Coolgardie to Esperance.

For the initial twenty-four
Are now a monster omnivore!

Seven eat as much as a sheep
And rabbits never oversleep.

Even facing grim starvation
Rabbits keep up procreation.

The government puts out a reward
For some technique to halt the horde.

Coleman Phillips earns some merits
When he lets out gangs of ferrets.

Some build a wall like that in China
Only longer and much finer.

Others hit on a brilliant plan
To stick the rabbit into a can!

Rabbits may be pestilential
But rabbit stew has great potential.

For those who put their creed in this,
Rabbit stew becomes big business.

At the height of the rabbit maraud,
Nine million cans are sent abroad.

Meanwhile States increase their prizes,
Hoping something materialises.

Of the thousands who have a go,
The one to find it was Aragao.

He sought the Pied Piper mixed with Moses,
What he got was Myxomatosis.

What a great man! His one big failure
Was not to do it in Australia!

For despite his good intention,
We took decades to use his invention.

The one to mend the fatal error
Was the dogged McNamara.

What a woman! She ignores all
Fear of chemical control.

Her research may cause kerfuffle
But the woman doesn't ruffle.

And so the virus that's terrific
Works its way across the Pacific.

McNamara's totally lost in
Undoing the harm of Thomas Austin.

Studies species, breeding habits,
Spurts the virus into rabbits.

Just when progress seems most static,
Comes a sudden change dramatic.

On the south-east Gippsland coast
Rabbits stumble round comatosed.

In nineteen fifty-one alone
Ten million die racked to the bone.

And as a reward for all their pain,
Jean McNamara is made a Dame.

WHEN THE FACE ON THE MONEY WAS HERE

1954

Don't you wish you'd been around
   In nineteen hundred and fifty-four
When a mystical experience
   Wafted over the Australian shore?

Menzies thought he'd teach the lefties
   A pretty basic thing or two,
And imported straight from London
   The freshly throned young QE2.

From Fremantle to Bundaberg
   Australia stood for weeks in queues,
Millions filed the streets in lines,
   And this before they'd port-a-loos.

All the papers published brochures,
   Everyone bought a souvenir,
A sudden thrill ran through the nation:
   The pretty face on the money was here!

Royalty now strolled among us
   The Queen and Prince within our sight,
It was real, it was stunning,
   The biggest thing since Vegemite!

The Petrov Affair
1954

Two years before the advent of television in Australia, one great source of family entertainment was following the Government's McCarthy-style pursuit of communists.

Sometime in Feb of Fifty-four
A Russian loses esprit de corps.

Has secret files, feels overchecked,
Contacts Aussies, wants to defect.

When PM Menzies hears of scheme,
Asks spy Petrov to hold his steam.

'The time's not ripe,' he tells the man.
For Bob has his own five-year plan.

Shrewd was Menzies, wise, hilarious,
A typically loudmouth Sagittarius.

Stalin was one, so was Franco,
And probably the ghost of Banquo.

Give them power and there's no reprieve,
Once they're in, they never leave.

Brezhnev was one too and so was Mao,
Once they're in, they can't say ciao.

And to keep power they are ready
To get involved in all things shady.

And since they're ruled by Jupiter
They'll snoop and sneak and monitor.

Though Bob did his machination
For the sake of this wacky nation.

For should Evatt run Canberra
It'll be nothing but Red Terror.

And as it seemed that Evatt might win
The PM swore to bring him ruin.

Here comes April, Menzies hell bent,
Makes a stagy speech in Parliament.

'We've got a spy who's spilled the beans:
Reds want power by any means!

'They've infiltrated Labor's lair,
There are Reds under beds everywhere!'

Evatt laughs it off as trivia,
Underestimates hysteria.

Petrov decamps, Russia blows fuse,
The world reacts with headline news.

KGB crossed, nabs wife Petrova,
But lose her in Darwin stopover.

Insults are swapped, Embassies close,
Names and faces the Petrovs expose.

The McCarthy era is in full swing,
People believe almost anything.

For lo and behold on the Petrovs' list,
Many a Labor activist!

What shock to read in the *Petrovgraph*,
The names of men on Evatt's staff!

How upsetting! What disrepair!
The Red, it seems, ARE everywhere.

So Doc Evatt may be a real good bloke,
But he doesn't even get to stroke.

Menzies wins, Evatt bats zero,
Petrov the traitor becomes the hero.

No one will the patriot believe,
They go for the lies the ratbags weave.

Menzies convenes a Royal Commission:
Labor melt-down, Party fission.

The Strange History of the Liberal Party

1916-1954

In nineteen sixteen
  With Labor in power,
Weedy PM Hughes,
  Is stud of the hour.

There follows a blue,
  Hughes breaks with Labor
Starts his own bloodline,
  The Nationalist caper.

Its members trot in,
  All ex-Labor smarties,
Or from the Free Trading
  And Protectionist parties.

By Hughes out of Labor,
  As a matter of course,
The Nationalists become
  A Federal force.

It's some years later,
  Labor's once more in power,
This time it's PM Lyons
  Whose stud dreams turn sour.

Treasurer though he be,
  He sobs into his fists,
Gets up one morning and
  Joins the Nationalists.

The Nats he rebreeds
  Enthusiastic and hearty,
Into the United
  Australia out
  of Nationalists out of Labor Party.

Lyons wins Government,
  Shores his defences,
But his big job's still pinched
  By ambitious young Menzies.

But once war begins
  Menzies loses control,
And has four years to plan
  A new party and goal.

So at Albury
  In speech pert and tarty,
He launches the Liberal
  Out of United
  Australia out of Nats out of Labor Party.

Inside Doc Evatt's Labor,
  Bart Santamaria
Now feels that the Communists
  Are the chappies to fear.

So with RC Groupers,
  He splits Labor in two,
Breeds the Democratic
  Labor Party out of Labor Party anew.

But Menzies is too strong,
  Santamaria too right,
So Libs and DLP
  Never come to unite.

Which is quite a pity
  Since each party phalanx
Needs, now and then, traitors
  To freshen its ranks.

Albert Namatjira

It's hard to imagine today the consternation Namatjira's artistry caused in Australia. When he died in 1959, aged fifty-seven, he was by far the best known painter in the land.

There was a man of double life,
Worked with paints to keep his wife.
His name was Albert, hers was Rube,
He painted pictures from a tube.

Yellow boulders, purple hills,
He sure hoped they'd pay the bills.
You could find no art sincerer,
And he signed them Namatjira.

When the art began to sell
Albert found a place to dwell.
When the pictures rose in price
The tax man came to get his slice.

Albert earned dough far and wide
But he shared it with his tribe,
For when they saw that he was flash
Hundreds relieved him of his cash.

Once the white world thought him grand
Albert wanted a piece of land.
They honoured him with laurel and palm
But wouldn't let him own a farm.

Albert bought his tribe drink on a large scale,
White folks objected and stuck him in gaol.
When he could no longer practise his art,
A deep sense of sadness broke his big heart.

Jorg Utzon and the Opera House

The Opera House was paid for with money raised from expensive lottery tickets. Construction began in 1959 and it seems to be still going on.

One concrete sail
  Grows on the sea
All is calm as
  Calm can be.

Two concrete sails
  Begin to show
Gently trouble
  Begins to grow.

Three concrete sails
  Are tossed about
Loudly Parliament
  Starts to shout.

Four concrete sails
  Rise on their own
Gone are builder,
  Architect home.

Jorg Utzon and the Opera House

Our Dawn

Dawn Fraser was 19 years old when she won her first gold medal at the Melbourne Olympics in 1956. Her performance at the 1960 and 1964 Olympics proved unique in sporting history.

When Dawn was just a little girl,
To be exact her age was five,
She learnt to swim from brother Don
Then went straight into overdrive.

She pushed herself ten k's a day,
While we others twiddled thumbs,
She swam her legs tied up with rope,
Or towing open petrol drums.

With will to win and to win well
She broke new records forty times,
She overcame herself and us,
One of nature's paradigms.

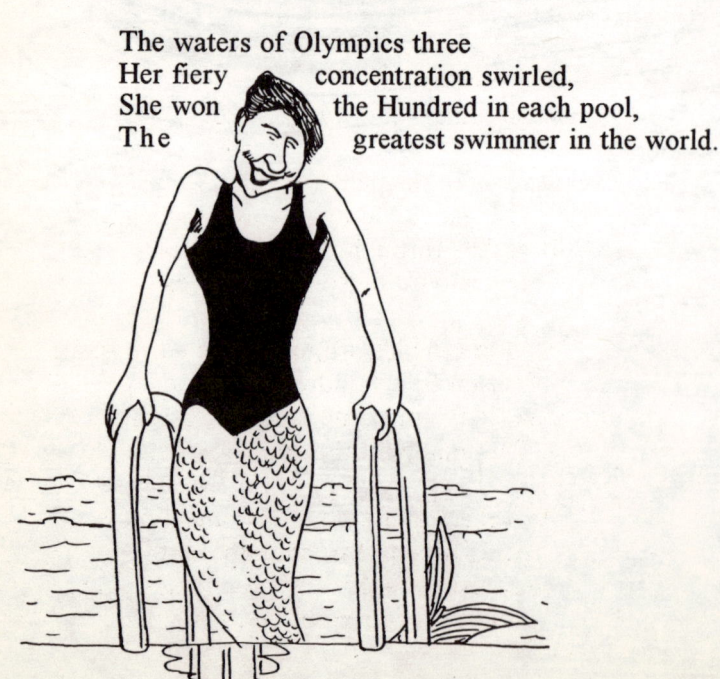

The waters of Olympics three
Her fiery concentration swirled,
She won the Hundred in each pool,
The greatest swimmer in the world.

The Snowy Man

Completed in 1972, the Snowy Mountains scheme is the greatest civil engineering project undertaken in Australia.

I was going up the Snowy
   With a couple of my folks,
I saw the biggest dam, mate,
   That was ever built by blokes.

This dam was really deep, mate,
   Deeper than the worst hangover,
Holds four quadrillion litres,
   Fills the Harbour eight times over.

The waters from this dam, mate,
   Drop down three thousand feet,
They stream down awesome tunnels
   That are wider than a street.

And deep inside these tunnels
   The water plummets in cascades,
It rushes through the mountains
   To drop on these giant blades.

And the blades are under the earth, mate,
   Buried four hundred metres deep,
And they spin around these turbines
   That make all this current cheap.

And the water spins the blades, mate,
   And fills up sixteen dams,
They use it to drench three states, mate
   In times of drought and jams.

Now the men who built that dam, mate,
    Spent half their life under earth,
And one of them was my dad, mate,
    Right round the time of my birth.

My bloody oath, it's the truth, mate,
    You didn't know that, I bet.
So next time you switch on the light, mate,
    You'll be burning a bit of his sweat.

The Vietnam War

1965 - 1972

There was a happy nation
   Thought she knew the score
Sent eight hundred men into
   A bloody Asian war.

The bloody Asian war
   Went longer than she thought
So the less than happy nation
   Sent four thousand for support.

The fresh support she sent
   Proved simply not enough
So then the nation not so happily
   Sent a Task Force to get tough.

But the Task Force that was tough
   Didn't spread round too much dread
So the scarcely happy nation
   Sent ten thousand troops instead.

The ten thousand troops she sent
   Just weren't enough to win,
And the seriously unhappy nation
   She went into a spin.

The spin she settled into
   Left her citizens in doubt
So the decidedly unhappy nation
   Decided to pull out.

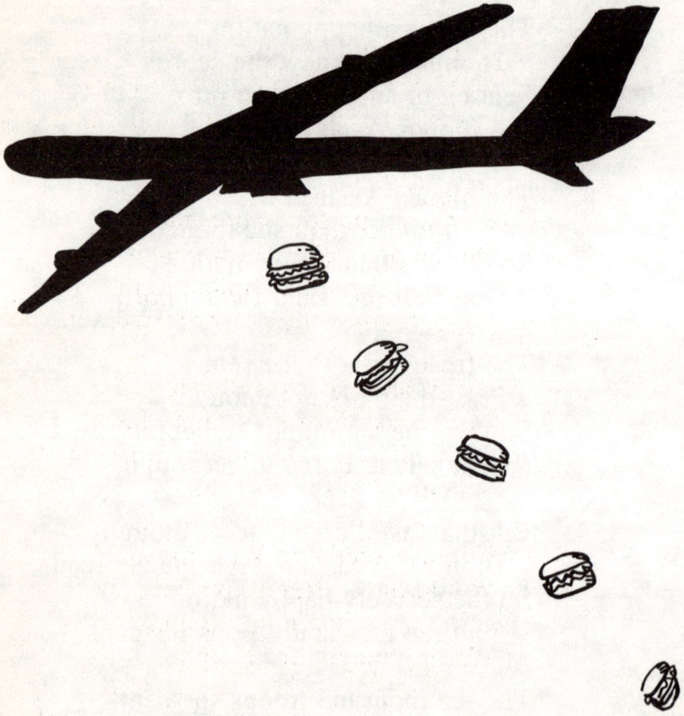

The Whitlam Sacking

Gough Whitlam became Leader of the Labor Opposition at the age of fifty, and Prime Minister six years later in 1972. Within three years he was to lose his position in unfortunate circumstances.

Seat in Senate becomes vacant
   State of Queensland must fill seat,
Labor's Whitlam hopes for good man
   Country Party has him beat.

Queensland places Labor-hater
   On the Senate's scarlet bench,
Who now gives the Opposition
   Enough votes the power to wrench.

Their procedure's very basic -
   Just block all of Whitlam's laws,
Continually for five months running
   Scheming in the corridors.

Whitlam were he in Westminster
   Would have offered to resign,
But in Oz he just hung in there
   Waiting maybe for a sign.

Then one bright November morning
   He gets Governor-General's sack,
And its swiftness is to Whitlam
   Like a Club across the back.

Full of moral indignation
   He fights hard to keep his job
Not realising that Australians
   Resent keenness at the top.

Certain of his moral rightness
   He knows he'll get back his gig
But voters hate his self-assurance
   And end up giving him the flick.

The moral of this story's simple
   And it really can't be missed:
Just don't admit you want your job
   And you'll never be dismissed.

The End of the White Australia Policy

1855 - 1976

In Eighteen-fifty
  The pop. was little,
The laws on migrants
  Non-committal.

With gold discovered
  The Chinese came,
And their successes
  Put Aussies to shame.

But Diggers adopted
  A rather dim view:
'They are so many,
  We are so few.'

They forced the laws
  To be re-written,
To keep out migrants
  Who weren't from Britain.

They kept this up
  For some six decades,
This tonguing of
  The barricades,

And seeing the land
  · As their holy see,
Urged a Keep Australia
  White policy.

The law was cunning
   As the jungle lynx,
It didn't specify
   'No Boongs - No Chinks.'

The way it worked,
   How they got finessed,
Was by a simple
   Dictation test.

Unwanted Asians
   Were ordered to pen
Fifty words in Dutch
   Or Hungarian.

It had to be veiled,
   The point was ticklish,
Because many spoke
   Quite fluent English.

The system worked,
   In Europe reigned fear
And so many people
   Aspired to get here.

But when the dust settled
   These whites came no more,
War refugee numbers
   Went right through the floor.

'Ah, what do we care,'
   Said Aussies all huff,
'We'll have to go coloured,
   There just aren't enough.'

And so in the Eighties
   With the pop. so little
The despised non-whites
   Received an acquittal.

The White Australia Policy

Of course it can't last,
  One day headlines will scream:
'Let's stop all this influx,
  Keep Australia Cream!'

The Dingo's Christmas

In December 1980, an inquest was held into the disappearance at Ayers Rock of a young baby girl called Azaria. The case became a national sensation.

By the Rock baby
   Sleeps in a tent,
Father's a shepherd,
   God knows where he went.

Mum's at the back,
   Making a cuppa,
The dingo's a guest
   And coming for supper.

Mother and child
   He sniffs from afar,
Crossing the desert
   He follows a car.

Right at the rock,
   No might be, no maybe,
Mm, thinks the dingo,
   I fancy a baby.

The desert is silent
   All the birds flown,
The tent's rent apart,
   The dingo's gone home.

Where is my baby,
   Cries fearful its Mummy,
Is it out in the desert
   Or in dingo's tummy?

The Dingo's Christmas

Hunters and coppers
  Get out on the track
But cannot seem able
  To bring baby back.

Judges and lawyers
  Sift through the sand,
But all that they manage
  Is to soil their hand.

Now roars a cyclone
  And darkens the sky
And a huge windstorm
  Blows everyone high.

Shepherd and wife
  Tumble round in the air,
Murkiness rages
  Everywhere.

That Year

What a year it was! What a spree!
There was no time like eighty-three!

Bob stopped drinking and got a job,
Mal went back to being a country slob.

While Ron still kept mumbling 'Giddy-up,'
Bondy snatched the America's Cup.

Luciano struck a chord,
And Caucus gave us The Accord.

Hoges kept on snarling 'G'day, mate,'
Sir Peter was pure dynamite.

Di and Charles decided to visit,
Hawthorn's play was just exquisite.

First reported case of AIDS,
ASIS made some stupid raids.

Enormous crowds for Charles and Di,
Cops kept searching for Don Mackay.

Sydney saw its biggest bust,
And Melbourne drowned in a storm of dust.

History was made by Four Corners,
Ayers Rock went back to its owners.

Bushfires raged all Ash Wednesday,
Queensland issued a flood Mayday.

The news was good, assured Barnard,
And everybody got a Bankcard.

Paul still had a long way to go,
And everyone still laughed at Joh.

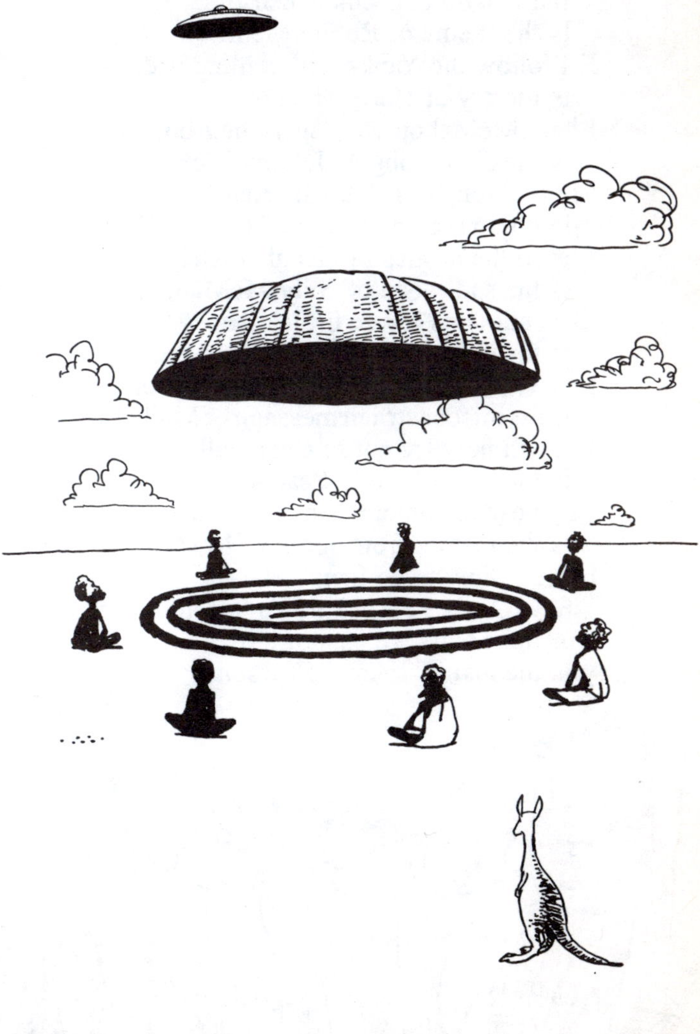

Liberal Leaders

John Hewson was elected leader of the Liberal Party in 1990. If pushed to the border, would you know his antecedents' order?

What Australia needs is censors,
    Is the theme of Robby Menzies.
I'd follow the Yanks with a blindfold,
    Is the cry of Harry Holt.
I hate McMahon with every neuron,
    Is the short song of Johnny McEwen.
My bad tongue I gotto shorten,
    Is the brave admission of Johnny Gorton.
I let in the hordes of Genghis Khan,
    Is the sad moan of Billy McMahon.
My balloon is a wee bit leaden,
    Is the swan song of Billy Snedden.
Life was meant to be lived in a blazer,
    Is the misconstrued message of Mally Fraser.
We will now try not to sleepwalk,
    Is the plea of Andy Peacock.
I'll show the unions I'm no coward,
    Is the refrain from Johnny Howard.
I forgot how to be firm,
    Says Andy Peacock in his second term.
Our tight belts we cannot loosen,
    Is the *gist* of Johnny Hewson.

Keating's Lament

*In 1991 Federal Treasurer Paul Keating
sadly resigned his position.*

Bobby, Bobby,
What is your hobby,
Where is your promise true?

He made me his bride
Then tossed me aside
And stole my front bench too.

The Twelve Sons of Mother Labor

*Paul Keating was elected
Prime Minister in December, 1991. He is the twelfth man to
lead the Labor Party since 1904.*

Good Mother Labor
  So feared plutocrats,
She sent out against them
  Her twelve little brats.

Her first born Watson
  She made him the chief,
But his raid on the world
  Proved stormy and brief.

Her second born Fisher
  She gave him three go's,
But he finished up leaving
  Over war and egos.

Her third born Hughes,
  Ambitious and small,
She kicked him outside
  After a brawl.

Her fourth born Scullin
  Was quiet as a mouse,
Yet in the end he nearly
  Brought down her house.

Her fifth born Curtin
  Was gentle of breath,
But somehow or other
  She worked him to death.

Her sixth born Chifley
  She never did spank,
But still he went crying
  All the way to the bank.

Her seventh born Evatt
  Was most loyal and true,
Until one day her home
  He split right into two.

Her eighth born Calwell
  Could have got far,
But she just cut his wings
  And said, 'You're a galah.'

Her ninth born Whitlam
  Was on top of her list,
But he had to leave home
  All sad and dismissed.

Her tenth born Hayden
  She put to the slog,
But one day she swapped him
  For a drover's old dog.

Her eleventh born Hawke
  Brought home the most bread,
But he ended up somehow
  Pushed out of the bed.

Her twelfth born Keating
  Just didn't like school,
But she smiling gently
  Said, 'You're the one who'll...'

DANCING THE MABO

1993

The dolphin claimed the land
   While the pig ate all the sand
The crocodile sat on the chair
   While the sheep flew through the air
The dingo said 'If you please?'
   While the shark ate all the trees
What the hell is going on here?
   Said the puzzled bottle of beer
Just give me half a chance
   And I'll teach you all to dance.

AUSSIE KEATING GOES A-CLEANING

1993

Aussie Keating goes to Britain
  And takes with him a parcel,
And hands it to the English Queen
  In her pretty Scottish castle.

Her Majesty at first is flattered
  But her smile soon turns to a frown
When in the cardboard box she finds
  Her somewhat squashed and tarnished crown.

'Oh, why is it so badly battered?'
  Asks Her Majesty in tears.
'Because we had it for so long,
  For at least two hundred years.'

'But we've trinkets five times older,
  Not that I wish to bicker.'
'Ah, but Majesty, Down Under
  They rust a helluva lot quicker.'

'But you should keep it anyway,
  Antiques do come of use.'
'It's much too much old-fashioned, Ma'am,
  The clasp's busted, the screw is loose.'

'Ah, well, never mind, my craftsmen
  Will soon hammer out the nicks.'
'Ma'am, I seriously doubt it,
  The thing is fast falling to bits.'

'Oh, I think you'll be surprised,
  We build our goods sturdy and strong.'
'That maybe so, your Majesty,
  But we've had this for far too long.'

The English Queen with disdainful look
  Flings the old crown in her trunk,
Aussie Keating goes home light-headed
  For having got rid of the junk.

The Pest Poem

1788 - 2000

This is the convict
  With gusto and zest
Kicked out of England
  For being a pest.

This is the Redcoat
  With musket and tail
Brought in to guard
  The convict in jail.

This is the cochineal bug
  Ground to a shred,
Brought in to make dye
  For the soldier's coat red.

This is the prickly pear
  Bristles all smug,
Brought in to feed
  The cochineal bug.

This is the landscape
  That once was so fair,
Completely consumed
  By the mad prickly pear.

This is cactoblastis
  Its hungry jaws set
Brought in to devour
  The prickly pear threat.

This is the wasteland
  Full of dead nasties,
Killed off completely
  By cactoblastis.

This is the cane
  That makes our tea sweet,
Grown on the ravaged land
  Out in the heat.

This is the brown moth
  Who knows the name,
That's flown in to feed
  On the poor sugar cane.

This is the cane toad
  Full of poison and sloth
Imported to swallow
  The sugar cane moth.

This is the motor car
  Out on the road,
Weaving around
  To squash the cane toad.

This is the driver
  Speeding possessed,
Here to smash cars,
  The ultimate pest.

Republic Bid 2000

When Sydney was awarded the Olympic Games for the Year 2000, the whole nation was gripped by a sense of excitement. Not wishing to be upstaged, Prime Minister Paul Keating submitted his own bid for the Third Millennium.

In nineteen hundred and ninety three
   Hands still tightly on the reins,
PM Keating makes a decision
   To bid for the Republican Games.

After an approximate costing,
   A makeshift model made to scale,
The ex-Treasurer feels certain
   His heart-felt bid just cannot fail.

He offers Australians at large,
   Ultimate judges of his bid,
A seductive presentation
   That now no longer need be hid.

'If your life's without rewards,
   If you're living just on schemes,
Now we've something to works towards,
   We'll pour concrete in our dreams.

'Now we will show the entire world,
   We'll become one big powerhouse and
Standing up on our own free feet
   Hold the Republican Games 2000!

'We'll turn the whole of Australia
   Into one humungous stadium,
For our Republican regalia
   Will run for a whole millennium.

'We'll wrestle with our identity
    And fence with iconoclastics,
We'll have synchronised flag-waving
    And political gymnastics

'We'll leap Presidential hurdles
    And pole-vault across the throne,
We'll run around in Asian circles
    And bravely dive through the unknown.'

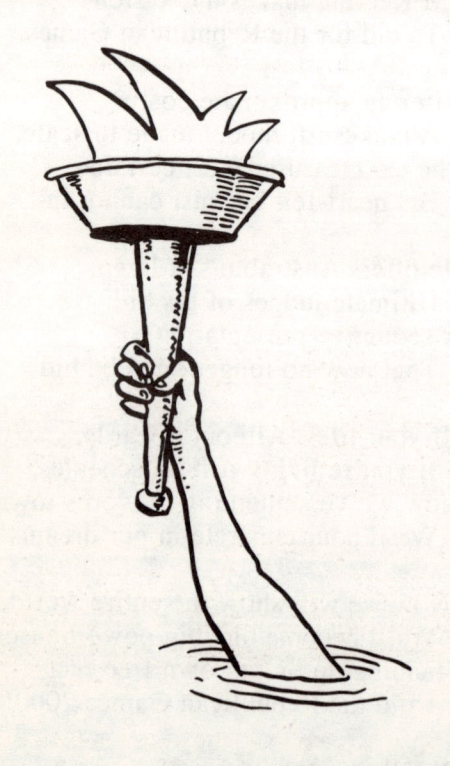

Anthem

To be sung to the **Aeroplane Jelly** *tune.*

I love Australia's cooee!
   Lucky Australia for me!
I love her beaut fauna!
   I love her esprit!
She never runs short
   Of a good repartee!
I love Australia's cooee!
   Lucky Australia for me!

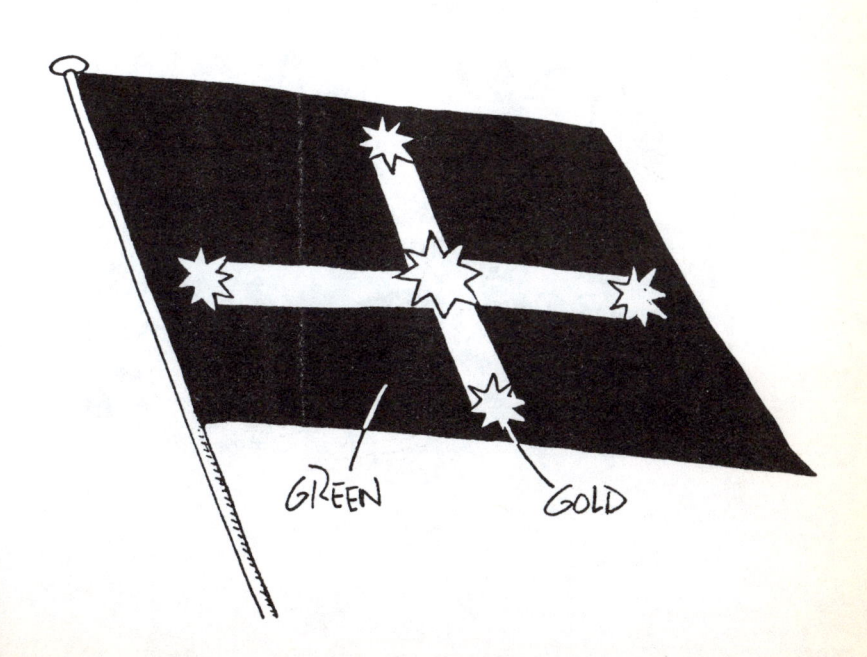

A Hop Through Australia's History